# Heathen Anthology Two

## by Valarie Wright

Wise Home 2007-2017

Wise Home Foundation #A-002

Published by Wise Home Foundation

Printed by CreateSpace, An Amazon.com Company

First bound edition

Cover Art by Valarie Wright

https://wisehomefoundation.com/

# Contents

# Heathen Anthology, Volume Two

Long before I wrote my first book, I was writing essays. At first, they were meant only for myself; similar to a diary, I was expressing my thoughts by journaling direct experience as I navigated academic journals, university libraries, and wild places, for any clue on or about the tradition of phenomenology that is Seidr.

This road is a familiar one, for I have been here before, delving into pre-history, because my memories of *Then* are as current as what I had for breakfast this morning. And because this subject is philosophical, mystical, and steeped in consciousness, it is misunderstood; even by those who claim to 'believe' and 'follow' these Old Ways.

Now I finish Volume Two – a journey I never imagined, all these decades past. Over these many years I have heard from untold folk how they remember my words, my essays, and how my books have "moved" them, have "informed" them, have "motivated" them to be .. that which they deeply *knew*, they were, all along.

The words I write fall deftly from my heart, the citations I note are numerous enough to keep even the most academically inclined amongst us busy for years, and the number of individuals who tell me they read my books with a "pad, pen, and marker" is indication that there are many who yearn to not just tread the surface of such matters, but delve deep the darkened depths.

The history of anthologies is that they have a cyclic nature, or that they develop in regular cycles. Rather like seasons that wax and wane, so too has the interest in these topics been as a tide in the mind of Heathenry. At times needed for its gain, and other times, best measured as a background for further growth in its future. In fact, editing my own essays – adding updated citations, correcting typographical errors, organizing my thoughts some ten or more years after they were first put to paper – I am reminded how some of these ideas were once considered 'not heathen'. I recall easily the consternation and condemnation some of these ideas received when first presented. Equally as there were forward-thinkers who 'knew', on an intuitive level, that this information was 'right' and 'triewe'. Indeed, there is nothing more faithful or steadfast then Halja, and the Hidden Earth Mothers. Little more enduring than Nerthus, and how mightful warriors laid down their weapons before her. Few topics more intriguing as Runes and Black Magic, let alone the adaptability of both after the Conversion.

In closing: I am part of a group that researches and implements the actuality of Seidr; one that recognizes Seidr as a philosophy. As such, we individually examine Orlog, to better determine which roots us and which fetters us. In that these three essays represent such an application of individual will, I hope they become guideposts upon your journey.

# Honoring Halja and the Hidden Earth Mothers:
## Exposing Christian Bias to Restore Familial Honor

## Introduction
The idea that the Old Europeans worshipped a sovereign, nurturing and maternal Earth Goddess is popular in neo-Paganism. Its adherents have generally accepted this idea as fact, and second-wave feminist scholars have written books on the Great Mother – whose alleged peaceful agricultural matriarchal societies were wiped-out or subjugated by nomadic marauding patriarchal tribes. Mostly these claims relate back to Hebrew or other desert clans who introduced brutal male gods to overthrow a primal divine mother.

Simply put, there is no evidence for such a hypothesis in any culture, nor any known society, at any time in history. Contrary to feminist and new age views, true matriarchy has never actually existed; there exists no historical record of any society in which women dominated (1). In truth, to limit powerful feminine influences to the role of peaceful and loving mothers is to deny their more complex and sophisticated nature; namely, beings quite capable of re-routing an enemies progression, of binding or cutting the fetters of war, of bloody vengeance and sacrifice (2). Certainly, not every mother is a queen or warrior, let alone goddess, or even a birth-giver for that matter; so to reduce all such figures as such is both insulting and ignorant. Likewise, to reduce all masculine influences to that of mindless warrior, brutal rapist, conniving thief, homosexual, or transvestite is equally degrading.

No doubt, a great deal has been, can be, and will be written on the role of women and Seiðbearers, female deities and Matrons, Gygjar and Goddess', but this essay is meant to be more concise – focusing on but one aspect of the feminine: the Hidden Earth Mothers.

## Huldrefolk
*Huldra* means 'hidden, covered'. In Old Norse *Hulda* is the name of a Gýgjar and means, 'cover, veil', and *huldu* means to 'hide, conceal'. In modern Scandinavian, the word is a noun used to describe a person, place, thing, quality, action, or function. So that someone can be *hulder* or a *huldrer*, and groups can be *huldrene*, *hulders*, and *Huldrefolk*.

In Germanic folklore the huldra are stunningly beautiful women, usually with long hair, who wear a *black veil* and frequent old groves or wells, caves or lakes (1). They are generally kind to human folk, bringing them blessings if they perform a prescribed task. Some myths relate how the huldra lure men to them for sex and procreation, to create a hybrid; then in return, reward them or kill them depending on the outcome. Generally speaking, there were three types of these hybrids, commonly known as *changelings*: those that were a human-fairy hybrid, those who were old fairies in disguise (mischief makers), and those that were inanimate objects (2). I refer here to the former. Children born of relations between humans and fairy/elves were known as *huldrebarn*, literally 'hidden children', or 'changelings' – who were originally considered blessings not banes, this latter being an idea the Church introduced. Huldrefolk are said to be excellent hunters and willing to help hunters who gift them a silver coin; likewise, they love animals and can cause cattle to give sweet milk or assure an easy birth for all farm beasts. It was the Christians who attached animal tails to them, sometimes horns, making them into half-human demonic creatures whose only intent was to do harm. Later still, Christian myth interpolated how Wodan hunted down and killed Huldrefolk during the Wild Hunt. Regardless of these lies, the Huldra remains highly regarded today, and akin to the dragon (which also suffered at the hands of the Church), is often depicted on coat of arms, family crests and national flags (3).

**Hidden Women**
Mostly, the huldra were considered 'hidden' and more often than not, portrayed as women. Today, some know these 'Hidden Women' by many names, such as: Hel, Hlodyn / Jord, Frau Holle, Huld, Hyndla, and Nehalennia – all ancient and wise-telling names deeply threaded to Old Norse, Old English, and Old High German *hel* and *helan* ('hide'). Considering the preconceived misconceptions regarding not just these women but what they represent, they deserve an updated and historically based re-evaluation.

_Hel and Halja_: Hel is both a place and a personification of place. Jacob Grimm referred to her as _Halja_, which he theorized as the Proto-Germanic form of her name. He further observed that: _"The higher we are allowed to penetrate into our antiquities, the less hellish and more godlike may Halja appear."_ (1)   Certainly, the oldest idea of Hel is as a realm of the dead, a place where folk go who have died on land, of an illness, or of old age; so following Grimm's linguistic example, I will refer to her as Halja, and her realm as Hel.

According to Germanic myth, once the dead are in Hel they are unable to physically return, so that "coming to Hel" in the _Eddas_ and _Sagas_ is a kenning for 'dying' (2).  Never in Germanic Mythology is Hel portrayed as a place of punishment, but merely the place where the dead reside.  The idea of Hel as a place of torment occurs in the Middle Ages, and again, is due to the Church's influence, as seen in the writings of both Snorri Sturluson and Saxo Grammaticus; both describe Hel as a place of suffering, making it akin to their Christian mythology.

Most information regarding Hel and Halja in modern Heathenry is based on Snorri's Christian-based descriptions, as found in _Gylfaginning_, such as:
-_Slider_, the 'weapon-bearing' river (_Völuspá_ 36), also known as _Geivimull_, 'spear bubbler' (_Grimnismál_ 27, _Gylfaginning_ 38).  Saxo claimed the latter to be a "border between the living and the dead".
-Wodan's journey to Hel in _Baldrs draumar_ and Snorri's account of Hermodr describes Hel as a "place of shadows" or, essentially, a fiery garbage dump (_Bible_, Luke 12, several passages).
-Snorri describes a three-headed dog that is said to guard the "gates of Hel", but in truth he was deliberately trying to compare Scandinavian Mythology to the then popular practice of relating folklore back to either Greek or Roman Mythology.  As such, Snorri placed Greek _Cerberus_ in Germanic Hel (_Baldrs draumar_ 3 and 4).
-_Helgrindr_, the fence around Hel, also known as _Nagrindr_, _Valgrindr_ or _Thrymgjoll_, has no relation to older Germanic myth; yet is related by Snorri in _Skírnismál_ 35 and in _Grimnismál_ 22; later, it was picked-up and added to _Lokasenna_ 63 and _Fjolsvinnsmal_. Essentially, Snorri relates that Hermodr cannot ride into Hel because he is alive, so he must jump the fence (_Gylfaginning_ 48).

-Snorri is the one who created the story about Halja being the daughter of Loki and Angrboda, sister to Fenris and Jörmungandr; which persists as an annoyingly glaring historical inaccuracy.

-Snorri is also the one who described Halja as "half black and half white"; a depiction that is found nowhere in Germanic Lore, but may be poetic (see below).

-In *Gylfaginning* 33, Snorri describes *Niflheim*, or the place where Halja is supposed to reside. Not only is his description virtually identical to Christian ideas of that age, but this information has mislead entire generations of Heathens by creating a whole new world with the stroke of a pen.

Snorri also created such absurd notions as:

-Halja's hall, *Elijudnir*, as "the damp place";

-Her plate and knife of "hunger";

-Her servant *Ganglati*, 'the slow one', and serving maid *Ganglot*, 'the lazy one';

-Her threshold as *falendaforad*, "stumbling block";

-Her bed and bed curtains as *kor* and *blikjanda-bolr*, "illness" and "bleak misfortune", respectively.

The fact that these descriptions are not considered original to either Germanic or Northern European mythologies, and that they clearly represent Christian allegory, and that every recognized scholar of Heathen Lore has shown them to be literary devices created by Snorri and Saxo, has not kept them from being believed – hook, line and sinker – by Heathens today (3). In short, these are infectious influences that must be eliminated.

So, what do we know about Hel and Halja? What is known and what is truly rooted in Germanic thought? First, to discern true Germanic Paganism, one must realize that polytheism and animism are at the forefront of ancestral thought, and that the Indo-European traditions are complimentary. What follows then are Heathen ideas, some of which are not mentioned until the Middle Ages, but mostly removed from Christian influence.

-The Road to Hel, as a realm, is reached by crossing the *River Gjoll*; meaning 'ringing, resounding, singing' river. (The bridge *Gjallarbru* is considered 'overly Christian', and was inserted by Snorri.)

-Hel is a realm of death, and is considered to be somewhere 'north', the same place where Jötuns make their homes (Heathenry's Wisdom-Keepers). It is perhaps best to understand this via the Celtic *Land of Women,* or *Tir na n'Og*, an Otherworld realm wherein the dead reside. Far from the Christian idea of 'fire and damnation', the Land of Woman was a place of sunshine and brimming health, of happiness and frith. In Western European megalithic burial mounds, entrance ways for the living are through the south and the body is placed in the north; which is the same north-south alignment that predominates in Bronze Age Ship Burials of the Vendel and Viking Age as well (Christian tradition buries the dead east-west). The Heathen orientation of north-south, has the body placed in the direction of the Winter Solstice, so the dead reside in the place of High Mindedness and Blessing, and upon rising, they will be facing the direction of the Summer Solstice, the direction of Rebirth and Vibrancy (where the living reside; 4). These celestial events signify 'death' and 'life', respectively. In all, this orientation indicates both a cult of the dead and a cult of the sun; or solar-life orientation rather than death-finality orientation (5).

-Hel is linguistically traced pack to Proto Indo-European *kel-, "to cover, conceal". At her beginning, she was *Kolyo*, 'The Coverer', and was a *source* or primary Goddess. Described as a "veiled woman", a "dark haired woman", her front-facing appearance is described as "beauty beyond compare", while her backside is the snow-covered yet fecund earth of a forest floor in winter – characterized by decaying leaves that 'cover' delicate tree roots, and of deep fungus that 'covers' sleeping mammals and reptiles alike. From a Proto-Dravidian translation by Hermann Güntert, Kolyo's realm is (6):

*Without summer and without winter,*
*without heat and without cold,*
*without struggle and without hunger,*
*without illness and without death.*

Which sounds remarkably similar to:

*Who is free from attachment, balanced in pleasure and pain //*
*Who is freed from anger, fear and anxiety //*
*Who is the same in cold and heat, and in pleasure and pain,*
*And who is free from attachment.*
-Bhagavad Gita 12.13-18
(This section of the *Gita* is guidance on not being afraid of death
or what comes after, and on the importance of
'listening' to divine wisdom)

The English word *hell* is directly from Old English, and further found in Gothic *halja*, and Old High German *helan*, all of which mean "to conceal, to cover". It is also found in Old Irish *cuile*, meaning "cellar"; which is why scholars have concluded that the idea of Hel – as the *realm of the dead* – originated with the *family grave* (Europe, megalithic, Stone, and Bronze Age graves; 7). Further, it is etymologically traced to such diverse names as Hindu *Kali*, Greek *Kalypso*, and Gaelic *Cailleach*. I have identified another possible reference from *Hyndluljóð* 33; namely *Svarthöfdi*, the "blackheaded one", who is the forebear of "all Seiðbereindr", or the Bearers of Seið (Keepers of Seið; Wisdom-Keepers).

-Halja, as a 'goddess', or the personification of death, is first seen in kennings from the 10$^{th}$ and 11$^{th}$ centuries. Such kennings include: 'the halls of Hel' (*salar Heliar*; *Völuspa* 43); and the 'house of Hel' (*rann Heliar*; *Baldrs draumar* 2).

*Hlodyn / Hlóðyn, Jörð*: Hlóð and hlóðynjar are Old Norse mythical and poetic names of "earth; hearth; fire place; homestead"; and Jörð is Old Norse and Icelandic for "earth" (further compare Faroese *jørð*, and Old English *eorðe*). According to *Völuspa* 56, Hlodyn is Donar-Thor's mother, and her name is found on five inscriptions in north and west Germany, and Friesland (1). In accord with current thinking, scholars consider Fjörgyn, Hlóðyn, and Jörð as synonymous; or, that all three relate the idea of 'earth'.

*Jörð* is an Old Norse Gygjar, or goddess, depending on the source material, which includes variations on her name. In Norse Eddic and skaldic poetry, for example, her name is given as *Fjörgyn*; examples of this are found in Old High German *furuh*, and Old English *furh*, both meaning 'furrow; ridge'. In Eastern Scandinavia, the earth goddess Fjörgyn was wed to Perkunas, the Lithuanian thunder god; according to Turville-Petre, this is a union of Norwegian and Balto-Slav folkways (2). According to Mallory, this would further identify her Indo-European origins (3). Notably, Frigg is also identified as Fjörgyn, as seen in Gothic *fairguni*, and Old English *fyrgen*, both meaning 'mountain'. Where the Old Norse sagas list upward of twelve or more goddesses (to include Jörð / Fjörgyn), the Old English consolidated that list and attributed the character of Mother Earth to Frigg – the young and beautiful bride of the *Vernal Pools* (1a).

Overall, as daughter of Nott/Night, Jörð is birthed from Darkness, so represents the primordial creative principle which lies teeming in unrealized, wild, and formidable places. Far-removed from the beaten path – both physical and mental – her imagery is obscure yet all-encompassing. Nor should this be considered a 'primitive' way of thinking, but acknowledgment of human reliance on 'her' as 'mother', or the primal source of life. As such, it is tempting to connect all earth mother imagery – from the Upper Paleolithic Venus figures (50,000 BCE), to the Neolithic female figures (10,000 BCE), to the Cucuteni-Trypillian female figures (5,500 BCE), or any of the literally thousands of womanly forms that have been found across Old Europe – to her. Yet, it remains presumptuous to assume that all these female figures give proof of her worship. Even so, the trail of belief in earth as a living being is, as Carl Jung relates, part of our *collective unconscious*. And though the idea of an Earth Mother has seemingly been with humans since prehistoric times – and she became recorded history in 1,500 BCE (3) – there remains only that gut sensation that she is indeed, our Mother, and so worthy of recognition. Certainly, the number of prayers, mantras, charms, and galdrs for a fruitful earth are beyond reckoning; and perhaps the most recognizable in the West is the Anglo-Saxon *Æcerbot* or 'Field Remedy':

> *Erce, Erce, Erce! Our Earth Mother!*
> *Give you – All-Wielder, Ever-Ruler –*

*Fields waxing full and wide-enriching.*
*Fertile and strong .. high shafts of swelling abundance!*
*Broad barley and spelt. White wheat and emmer.*
*All your expansive goodness!*

Compare:

*O Prithvi! Truth, High and Potent Law,*
*the Consecrating Rite .. Fervour! Queen of all that is!*
*Lady of the earth's four regions,*
*in whom our food and corn-lands had their being,*
*O Earth, may we recline on thee who bearest strength,*
*increase, portioned share of food, and fatness.* (3)

Grimm saw in 'erce' a goddess name, one he wrote as *Eorce*, or 'earth'; and others have speculated that she was a tribal Old English goddess. Perhaps, her incomprehensible nature and unsurmountable further reaches is also what makes Frigg so appealing – for the Vernal Pools are more immediate and accessible, then the ineffable Jörð. Whatever the case, Jörð, Prithvi, Cybele, Mat Zemlya, Gaia, Natura, Eorthe, Terra, all exist today as personifications of Mother Earth, our collective mother.

*Holle, Frau*: Frau Holle, <u>Huld/Hulda</u>, Hlodyn, and <u>Hludana</u> seem to all be either: related to each other linguistically, or by function. In fact, these names are so close in language and function that they could easily reflect time period changes. Holle's name – from Old High German and Modern German, to Danish and Icelandic, to Old English – means 'gracious, grateful; fair, kindly; faithful, loyal, true, devout'; and older still, from Proto-German and Proto Indo-European, 'favorable, gracious; inclined towards'. Certainly the Romans saw something familiar in her as Hludana, citing her blessings and attributes on five offering stones, from Spain to Frisia (1).

As Huld/Hulda, her name includes a meaning of 'hidden; cover; secret', and is related to both Holle (Frau) and huldra/huldru; this latter is found, again, in Huldrefolk or 'hidden folk'. If so, Hulda may be the ruler or 'queen' of these hidden-earth folk, which could mean the dead in general (making this another name for Hel/Helja). Regarding any relation to an Earth Mother, her name may also be notable in association with Seiðr; specifically as seen in *Huldra saga*, a text only mentioned in *Sturlinga saga*, and is now lost to us. It is tantalizing, if not sad, to consider this a missing manuscript detailing the female wisdom traditions among Völvas and Gýgjars (a common combination; 2).

No doubt, the female guardian in Old European lore is ancient; so that, as a Heathen history researcher and woman, I cannot help but wonder at the womb as a dark and hidden cave that we not only emerge from, but seek to return to as a source of wisdom. We do, after all, live upon the Earth's womb, draw nourishment from her fecund belly, raise our families upon her firmament, and return to that soil for growth and renewal. Either way, in that this name-form has remained until present day, it is safe to assume that the idea or function behind her name is still viable within the Heathen Weltanschauung.

*Hyndla* is both a Völva and Gýgjar, and if the tale named after her – *Hyndluljóð* – is any indication, she is no friend of Freyja. Her name is generally rendered as 'little dog; bitch', but linguistically, it is not that simple. Hyndla is found in Old Norse *hund*, and variously means 'hundred and hundred-fold (denoting 'much'); very wise or dog-wise (cunning); watch dog and deer hound; hunter'. In her poem, she is said to dwell within a cave, to ride atop a wolf, and is sought-out as a Wisdom-Keeper; this latter a role I have long contended is integral to that of Völva. According to Jere Fleck, *Hyndluljóð* is a cult poem, or an epic poem that elucidates both the mythical and historic past of a particular tribe or region (1). In any event, *Völuspá*, *Hyndluljóð*, *Gróagalðr*, and *Fjǫlsvinnsmál*, all seem to represent **Völva Mythology** (2):
-*Völuspá*, 'Sayings of the Seeress',
-*Hyndluljóð*, '(Magic) Song of Hyndla',
-*Gróagalðr*, 'Groa's Incantations', and
-*Fjǫlsvinnsmál*, 'Many Sage Speeches; Wise Magic Sayings'.

Hyndla, akin to other such Wise Women, is defined as either sitting atop a mound, buried in a mound, or residing in a cave. Both mounds and caves resemble each other, and carry similar imagery: a concealed sacred center or assembly point. Throughout Old European lore, both the mound and cave are meeting places of wise- and cunningfolk, gods, ancestors, and otherworldly beings. The linguistic similarity between German *höhle* (cave) and *hölle* (cover, conceal), cannot be denied. All these are correlations enough to confirm Hyndla's role as a Hidden and Holy Woman.

*Nehalennia* is an ancient goddess, dating to the 2d century BCE; she is a Germano-Celtic Matron/Mother mentioned in numerous votive altars. In Denmark, she had three dedicated temples, and twenty-eight votive stones, bearing her image and name, have been found; as such, she is far from the 'minor goddess' many have tried to portray her as. At her temple remains in Domburg and Colijnsplaar, there have been found enough tree stumps to suggest that they were surrounded by a 'sacred grove' (1). Likewise, a similar number of inscriptions have been found across Germany and Austria, Switzerland, and France, making for a total of 160 votive alters.

Nehalennia is often depicted with baskets of fruit or grain, a dog, and sometimes a ship; in Old European symbology:
-fruit and grain represent origin and fertility, potentiality and the mystic center;
-dogs represent wisdom and death, loyalty and faithfulness, companionship, cunning wisdom and guardian of the same (again, a Wisdom-Keeper); and
-ships represent more than seafaring, but navigation through life – or living in order to transcend, the Eternal Return, and the Holy Isle.
Notably, all these symbols can be related back to *Isis*, whom the Romans honored with alters when they occupied Lower Germania. Tacitus mentions the Germanic Isis and concludes that she is associated with the cult of Nerthus.

There is no agreed upon linguistic information regarding her name. Some suggestions have been: 'tides; water'; 'new moon, dark moon'; 'underworld, hell'; 'the giver, provider'; Latin *necare*, 'to kill'; Sanskrit *naraka* 'underworld'; Greek *nekués*, 'spirit of the dead', and the 17th century suggestion from Dr. Henrik Cannegieter, 'new, river, goddess' (2). Using a combination of sources, I too would like to contribute a suggestion:

-*ne*, 'near'; *neðan, neðo*, from both Proto-German and -Celtic, 'grant safety; might; strength; to offer protection; mercy, favor'. From Old High German and Proto-Celtic, *nebula*, meaning 'mist; fog; vapor'. Likewise, Proto Indo-European and Proto-Celtic *\*nect(-e, o-)* meaning 'death, placing after death'.

-*neamh*, from Irish and Welsh. Though modern language origins, I would be remiss to not include this option, which means 'cloud; fog'.

-*nifl-*, as in Germanic *Niflheim*, the realm of 'dark, fog', or the 'Home of Darkness'. This root is cognate with *Nibelung* or the German *Nibelungen* (Old Norse *Niflung*), a royal lineage/family. This would connect Nehalennia to the Franks of the Middle Rhine region, which certainly coincides with the locations of her temples and votive stones. To further support this idea, Tacitus mentions the *Nabalia River*, which was associated with cult worship.

-*\*nihw-ela / \*nehal*, of Proto-Germanic origin relates 'destroy; death; fate', this latter implying an Indo-European trinity (as in the Norns or Moirae).

-*haljo, halja*, 'holy, sacred; concealment, to cover'.
-*helan*, Proto-Germanic 'hide; hidden'

-*ennia*, 'woman; maiden'. Likewise, Indo-European *\*nei* meaning 'leading; helmsman; leader to safe harbor'. *–ennia* may also be a Roman corruption of a Celtic Mother: *Anu / Annie* (who is also associated with dogs), her name meaning 'to flow; good; god'.

In toto, these meanings could be: 'Holy Mother of Death', 'Protective God-Woman', and/or 'Dark Home Goddess'. Certainly, all these roots have etymological explanations that are mutually complementary, portraying Nehalennia as the personification of watery fertility, and wyrd/fate goddess of death. Further, her date in the archeological record indicates that she may have **preceded** Nerthus, perhaps even being a template for her (3, 3a). Then, for additional confirmation, Hendrik Wagenvoort describes her primary center of worship – Domburg (Amsterdam) – as the location where the 'souls of the dead journeyed on their way to the west' (4). As such, this places Nehalennia firmly on this list of Hidden Women.

Finally, a consideration I rarely see mentioned in research on this topic: That Tacitus related this Germanic Suebi goddess to the *Roman Isis*. Not the Egyptian or Greek Isis, but how the Romans understood her. Notably, there were 'Harbors of Isis' along both the Arabian and Black Seas – areas where the Vanir may have originated. And, per Plutach, a statue dedicated to her read:

*I Am All that has been, and Is, and Shall Be.*
*My robe no mortal has yet uncovered.*

To the Romans, Isis was a primary Mother Goddess, an Originator or Original God. She not only forged great weapons of might for warriors, but watched over them in combat, and escorted them to her realm upon death. She was portrayed as a Creatrix and psychopomp whose Flowing Primeval Waters give birth to All That Is, and whose symbols include both weapons of war and looms.

**Earth Mother**

*Jörd* means "earth" in Old Norse – she is considered both a goddess of the Æsir and a Gýgjar; wed to Wodan and mother to Donar-Thor (1). According to Snorri's rendition, she is also the daughter of Nótt, "night", and has a second husband named Anarr (*Gylfaginning* 9). The name Jörd is ancient, and many scholars have considered that the names Fjorgyn, Hlodyn, Fold, and Grund, can either be synonyms with Jörd or Earth Mothers in their own right. An idea that certainly needs to be considered is that all these names reflect tutelary and/or tribal entities.

Indian mythology relates that Indra – Donar-Thor's Indo-European counterpart – was born of a union between Father Sky and Mother Earth. This is akin to the Germanic proto-ancestor Tuisto (mentioned by Tacitus), and no less than that which is related in the *Eddas*; namely, that Bestla, a Gýgjar, is mother to Ódr, Vili and Ve, the 'gods' themselves. But, are all these entities truly gods/goddesses? Tacitus, writing in *Germania*, listed many Germanic 'gods', equivocating them, for the most part, with his interpretation of their Roman counterparts – so that Wodan became Mercury, Donar-Thor became Hercules, and Tyr became Mars. In the case of the goddesses, the Romans labeled them as 'matrons' or *mothers*, indicating tribal mothers or beings particular to a certain place and people. With this in mind it is important to realize that Tacitus also related that the Germanic tribes honored "their divine ancestors", and that the three major tribes – the Herminones, Ingaevones and Istaevones – were all descended from "divine ancestors". So do Heathens have gods or ancestors? Or, do the ancestors become gods? If so, which ones become gods and how do they become gods?

**Ancestor Veneration**
According to Scandinavian mythology, from Old Norse sources, these 'gods' are divided into two families:
-The Æsir, who generally represent strength and government, and
-The Vanir, who generally represent fertility and magic.
In the later Heathen and early Christian poetry, both Snorri and Saxo deified heroes like Bragi and Hermodr – literally, making them gods with the stroke of a pen. So that, apart from the oldest Old Norse examples of Wodan, Donar-Thor, Tyr, Frigg, Frey, Freyja, and Ullr, very few others were actually considered 'gods' until much later, when Christians began re-writing Heathen lore. So the question becomes: "*Were these gods, or were they great leaders who became protectors and defenders of their tribes, and so 'ancestors' of many?*" If Heathenry is truly an ancestral-based folk faith, then these questions, and several more, need be considered.

Ancestor Worship is an idea based on the belief that deceased family members have a continued existence, take an interest in the affairs of their family's life, and are able to influence family members. These practices are *not* to be confused with the ritual significance of dying and death found in other world cultures (some differences are addressed below). The goal of ancestor worship is to ensure the ancestors' continued well-being and positive disposition towards the living, and sometimes ask them for assistance. The social or non-religious function of ancestor worship is to cultivate kinship values like respect, loyalty, and continuity of family lineage; an example of which is seen in the *fetch/fylgja*.

Though not a universal practice, ancestor worship or veneration is found in varying degrees of social and political construct, and remains a vital component of various religious practices in modern times. In those cultures that practice ancestor worship, this is different from worship of gods. Gods, for example, are attached to local temples, and are asked for favors. Generally speaking, ancestors are not asked for favors, but asked to *do their family duty* – which is to watch over their *lineage*. Some cultures believe that ancestors need to be provided for by their descendants; while others do not believe the ancestors are aware of them, but that expressing family duty is.

For those unfamiliar with how ancestor worship is actually practiced and thought of, the use of the word 'worship' can cause misunderstanding, and in many ways, is a misnomer. In English, the word *worship* originally meant the 'condition of being worthy; honor, renown', so can apply to both an ancestor or a divine being. However, ancestor worship does not mean that a departed loved one has become deified, rather, that they are recognized and respected, and their guidance in family matters can be sought. Many cultures today practice ancestor worship by visiting the graves of deceased loved ones, leaving flowers for them on family alters, or simply remembering them. As such, 'ancestor veneration' is the modern vernacular that expresses best how ancient Heathens thought of their dead – which was *worshipful*, or 'full of worth; worthy'.

The countries commonly associated with ancestor worship/veneration are Oriental – China, Japan, and Vietnam. However, ancestor worship/veneration is deeply rooted in Indo-European practices, so found not only in India but many European countries as well. For example:

-in Germany and Austria, at All Saints Day;
-in Ireland, at Samhain and Christmas Eve, where food is left outdoors; and
-in America at Easter, Christmas (Yule), Imbolc (Disting and Disirblot) and Halloween (All Soul's Day/Winter Nights).

Likewise, roadside shrines that mark the location of a loved one's death in a traffic accident, could be deeply residing remnants of ancestor veneration.

**The Coverers**

Do ideas like Hel as a female figure who resides over the realm of the dead deserve to be recognized? In that death is a universal concept and that several ancient cultures worldwide have honored the dead and death goddesses, it seems only fair to reconsider Hel's role at the high table. And if Hel is considered a goddess, then could burial mounds – which were well-known places of worship and sitting-out – be viewed as 'maps of the underworld'? (1) There is no doubt that:

-Bryn Celli Ddu ('Mound of the Dark Grove'), and Barclodiad y Gawres ('Giantesses' Apron) in Wales,
-Newgrange (Brú na Bóinne, 'Temple of Boanne') in Ireland,
-West Kennet Long Barrow in England,
-Hünengrab ('Stone, Hidden Grave'), in Germany,
-Carnac (La Trinité-sur-Mer, 'Kingdom of the Undersea), in Brittany; and many, many others, were both burial mounds and centers of worship, where many tribes congregated. And in virtually every instance, there is well documented proof that these sites were built to accommodate ritual processions – meaning huge crowds (social coordination), ritual ceremonies (Godwise (2), priestly cast), and possible cosmological outlines (most of these sites are linked with celestial movements). To further support this idea, in 2009, *Annwn*, the Celtic Land of the Dead, was located in North Wales – according to ancient surveyor maps; specifically, beneath the Ruabon and Halkyn Mountain ranges (3).

So if burial mounds were more than simply places to put the dead, but places to 'cover' and 'hide' them, to better protect them and/or afford them passage to Hel or the 'other world', equally as locations to visit loved ones, and converse with them, then this meant that they were sites of long-standing occupation, participation, and celebration. As such, this idea lends itself to reconsidering the role of Hel within Heathenry.

## Dead But Not Gone

Can the prevalence of so many names for female figures who 'cover' or 'hide' or are the 'earth' itself, coupled with burial mounds and megalithic passage tombs give us a glimpse into how our ancestors considered death and the realm of death? Yes, it can. Certainly, having settlements with a central focal point, such as a large earthen mound, would have been more than a center of tribal activity and ritual worship, but possibly an outline of Heaven and Hel. The dead are, after all, legitimate and contributory aspects of our personal experience in that they continue to influence our lives; a role that may have an impact on our current social and political concerns as well. Finally, if the dead where 'hid' or 'covered' in a mound that opened to another realm, and because the living visited these places, then can Hel or her hall be all that bad?

~ ~ ~

## Reference

**Honoring Halja and the Hidden Earth Mothers: Exposing Christian Bias to Restore Familial Honor**
Written in 1998, revised 2008, 2015, and 2017. Presented at 'Lunch and Lore' (a monthly meeting of area Heathens in central Georgia); at Southlands Moot (a regional Georgia moot); and at Florida Moot, in 2008. Presented at the Gathering of Asatru and Pagan Women (2015, Missouri); and at Savannah Pagan Pride (2015; Georgia). In Europe: Presented at the Weida Konferenz, Bodensee, Germany, 1998; and at a Sami Noaide reunion, Finland, 2007.

**Introduction**
1-J. M. Adovasio, Olga Soffer, and Jake Page, *The Invisible Sex: Uncovering the True Roles of Women in Prehistory*, 2007, pages 251-255.

2-Folke Strom, *Diser, Norner, Valkyrjor*, 1954, throughout, and pages 32-49

**Huldrafolk**
1- *Svarthöfdi* meaning "blackheaded one", from *Hyndluljóð* 33, so that all Seiðbereindr, or 'bearers of seið', can trace their lineage to the 'blackheaded one'.
Wright, V., *Old Europe's Seið-Bearers: Their Mythic Origins and Lineage*, 1989.

2-W.Y. Evens Wentz, *The Fairy-Faith in Celtic Countries*, 1911 (1981 republication), page 179-181.

3-Huldra banner.  One such example is the County Vestfold flag, in Norway.  Likewise, the Welsh national flag depicts a dragon.

**Hidden Women**
*Hel and Halja*
1-Jacob Grimm, *Teutonic Mythology*, 1882 (2004 republication).

2-Coming to Hel, and dying.  According to Heathen lore, the body does not return but the soul, or an aspect – possibly the *fetch* – does return.

3-Several scholars.  Namely, De Vries, Chadwick, Davidson, and Simek.  Also, Oscar Almgren, *Hallristningar och kultbruk*, 1927 academic paper, throughout.

4-Attributes of the celestial and terrestrial observances are the author's inherited heritage and culture, attitudes, sentiments, and ideals within her multi-generational family system. Therein, several individuals are recognized as *Keepers*, who are entrusted with the responsibility of preserving and passing-on the beliefs, observances, and traditions. Researching these family traditions, the author has discerned that Keepers are meant to 'care for and heed the innermost wisdom', which is exact from an etymological perspective. 'Keep' is found in Old English, from Proto-German *kopjan, so its meaning – and role – are ancient; overall it means one who is tasked "to observe, to carry out in practice; to regard, to pay attention to; to observe; to guard, defend, to preserve, to secure".

5-North-South orientation. Reference *Heathen Anthology, Volume One*, essay one: *Aurgelmir and the Four Dwarves: Sacred Center and Four Directions*, 2017.

6-Hermann Güntert, *Kalypso, Bedeutungsgeschichtliche Untersuchungen auf dem Gebiet der indogermanischen Sprachen*, 1919. Güntert is still regarded as an imminent scholar of Malayalam language, specifically his work on how it diverged from Proto-Dravidian. His translations were taken directly from ancient copper and stone tablets from languages pre-dating Sanskrit. (He is the also the grandfather of Hermann Hesse.)

7-Realm of the Dead.  It's interesting to speculate on the findings at Göbekli Tepe (11,500 – 6,000 BCE), where the heads of the dead have been found richly adorned, decorated, and buried beneath the hearth stones of individual homes.  At Çatalhöyük (7,500 – 5,700 BCE), where multiple bodies were buried within the home; then the same practice among the Sumerians (3,000 BCE).  The idea of keeping (presumably) loved ones nearby, over so many thousands of years, leads one to consider a worshipfully detailed cult of the dead.  Klaus Schmidt, the German archaeologist and pre-historian who led the excavations at Göbekli Tepe, speculated that *"First came the temple, then the city."*  Following the Indo-European migration into Europe, and the 63 individuals buried at Stonehenge (3,000 BCE) may be considered in a new light – a Seið-shamanesque one.  Professor Schmidt certainly thought as much, in two Papers: *Göbekli Tepe: Eine Beschreibung der wichtigsten Befunde erstellt nach den Arbeiten der Grabungsteams der Jahre 1995–2007*, and *Erste Tempel – Frühe Siedlungen: 12000 Jahre Kunst und Kultur, Ausgrabungen und Forschungen zwischen Donau und Euphrat*.  He speculated on this site representing a shamanic temple, complete with T-shaped pillars covered in animal reliefs as 'guardians' of the dead within.  Ideas concurred upon by scholars who compare the corresponding beliefs of Sumerian Mythology, and its sacred mountain *Ekur*, inhabited by ancient gods and surrounded by fierce beasts.

*Hlodyn / Hlóðyn, Jörð*:
1-Detail regarding Hlodyn: *Völuspá: Seiðr as Wyrd Consciousness*, Valarie Wright, 2005, pages 127 and 148.
1a-Vernal Pools. *Voluspa: Seidr as Wyrd Consciousness*, pages 86, 102, 116, and 122.

2-Turville-Petre, E.O.G., Myth and Religion of the North, page 97, 1964

3-Mallory, J.P., *In Search of the Indo-Europeans: Language, Archaeology and Myth*, page 129, 1989.

3-*Prithvi Sukta*, from the *Atharva Veda* 12.1-63.

*Holle, Huld, Hludana:*

1-*Corpus Inscriptionum Latinarum*, a comprehensive collection of ancient Latin inscriptions.

2-Huld. *Ynglinga saga* and *Sturlunga saga*.

## *Hyndla*

1-Fleck, Jere., *Konr, Óttar and Geirröd: A Knowledge Criterion for Succession to the Germanic Sacred Kingship*, 1970, page 48-65.

2-Völva Mythology. A coined phrase by the author to give name to the Eddas, sagas, and folk tales that may have been written either by Seiðwomen, or detail and/or define their role, function, and practices.

## *Nehalennia*

1-Busuijen, G., *Rodanum: A Study of the Roman Settlement at Aardenburg and its Metal Finds*, paper, 2008.

2-Cannegieter, H., *Groot Gelders Placaet Boeck*, 1740 (a Dutch Law Book).

3-Stuart, P., *Apples Are Not Unique to Nehalennia: The Mother Goddess*, page 91, 2003. And, van Boxhorn, M., text notes: Nehalennia, Leiden 1647, as noted in Dekker, C., *The Origins of Old Germanic Studies in the Low Countries*, page 209, 2007.
3a-Nehalennia as Nerthus. Desmond, Y., *Nerthus: Our Germanic Goddess of Death and Tribal Blessing*, 2007

4-Wagenvoort, H., *The Journey of the Souls of the Dead to the Isles of the Blessed*, pages 274-280, 1971 (reprint).

## Earth Mother

1-Mother to Donar-Thor. *Haustlong* 14; *Thrymskvida* 1; *Lokasenna* 58; *Gylfaginning* 37; *Skaldskaparmál* 4.

## The Coverers

1-Hel as a goddess. Can a deity be a primal human concept, such as death, life, and life in death?

2-Godwise, akin to "godhead", used to denote wise and self-recognized / realized / enlightened Seiðus. *Seidhr Sprehhan: The Sayings of Seidhr*, V. Wright, 2016, found throughout.

3-Land of the Dead; Ruabon and Halkyn Mountain range. Ruabon Mountain was originally known as Mabon Mountain. Mabon is the "Divine Youth" and hunter of the sacred boar Twrch Trwyth. His mother is Matrona, the "Divine Mother". Significantly, nearby, is a small village called 'Holywell Common', where, there exists a holy well and a "bottomless lake" (the latter is according to locals). This is also the site of Saint Winifred's Well, which has been called the "Lourdes of Wales", or a central place of healing and renewal.

# Nerthus: A Germanic Goddess of Death and Tribal Blessing

## Introduction

In 2007 I attended an Asatru / Heathen Moot where I was invited to attend a Nerthus ritual. Knowing that such a rite historically called for a human sacrifice, I was intrigued as to how this would be carried-out. A local "seidwoman" had crafted a small wagon (Radio Flyer) using craft paper and art supply items, complete with a doll adorned to represent Nerthus (that was hidden beneath a veil). A few words were spoken and the gathered folk were asked to follow "in silence", as we walked down a sandy road skirted on both sides by dark lake-fringed swamps and knobby cypress stumps. We arrived at a seemingly random location (the group was told "This is good enough"), where the officiant spoke about Nerthus and "her need for a sacrifice". This was que for a young man to step forward, who was identified as "willing to give his life" to the goddess. The officiant then stepped into the water, asked the young man to join her, where she rather clumsily dunked him underwater. My first impression was that of a Christian immersion baptism. As soon as the 'sacrifice' rose from the murky water, the officiant declared: "Ok, that's it. It's over. You all can go back to camp now." As anticlimactic as this was, upon returning to camp I learned that this was the third year for this rite, and that every year there had been a different officiant. Curious, I was also told that all three had experienced a series of "accidents", and that none were known to have fully recovered (car accidents and job loss, multiple personal injuries and hospitalization, bankruptcy and foreclosure); and as unpleasant as these sound, the 'sacrifices' had met with worse fates.

Back at camp, my host asked for my thoughts. I paused for a moment, then asked if anyone there was familiar with *Gautreks saga*. Only a few were familiar with the tale, and only vaguely; most had never heard of it. There, beneath a clear dark sky awash in starshine, I related the tale of King Vikar, and the lot of those who try to escape sacrifice. Specifically, how a thread's width of gut became a hanging rope and a thin reed became a hardened spear. As muggy afternoon air turned to dark Southern night, I finished speaking, and saw many a head nod in deep thought. Several months later, my dear friend contacted me, relating the sad details of the young man who had 'willingly' volunteered to be 'sacrificed' that day, and that the next moot would need a new officiant. I was asked of my interest as officiant, and my reply was that more research was needed before such an undertaking. That was when I began investigating Nerthus for this essay, and experimenting with *prolonged self-sacrifice*.

What follows are my discoveries and revelations of this remarkable, little understood, and possibly underappreciated goddess. In this essay's final section – *Part Last: Creating a Modern Heathen Nerthus Rite* – I have included a workable outline for a modern-day *self-sacrifice*; a format that myself and a close friend (a dedicated Vitki) tried and tested upon ourselves (runic peorth). My self-sacrifice was to Helja, and his to Wodan. We created detailed and challenging tasks that we Oathed to carry-out over the course of a year. Twelve tasks completed – and now, more than a decade later – both of us have had sweeping success in all our endeavors; so no ill-effects. This essay then, can be read to learn more about Nerthus, or as a springboard for a personal, a family, or a kindred dedication; the choice falls to the reader.

## Part One: Chapter 40

The Langobardi, on the other hand, are ennobled by, the smallness of their numbers; since though surrounded by many powerful nations, they derive security, not from obsequiousness, but from their martial enterprise. The neighboring Reudigni, and the Avions, Angli, Varini, Eudoses, Suardones, and Nuithones, are defended by rivers or forests. Nothing remarkable occurs in any of these; except that they unite in the worship of Hertha, or Mother Earth; and suppose her to interfere in the affairs of men, and to visit the different nations. In an island of the ocean stands a sacred and unviolated grove, in which is a consecrated chariot, covered with a veil, which the priest alone is permitted to touch. He becomes conscious of the entrance of the goddess into this secret recess; and with profound veneration attends the vehicle, which is drawn by yoked cows. At this season, all is joy; and every place which the goddess deigns to visit is a scene of festivity. No wars are undertaken; arms are untouched; and every hostile weapon is shut up. Peace abroad and at home are then only known; then only loved; till at length the same priest reconducts the goddess, satiated with mortal intercourse, to her temple. The chariot, with its curtain, and, if we may believe it, the goddess herself, then undergo ablution in a secret lake. This office is performed by slaves, whom the same lake instantly swallows up. Hence proceeds a mysterious horror; and a holy ignorance of what that can be, which is beheld only by those who are about to perish. This part of the Suevian nation extends to the most remote recesses of Germany.

-Tacitus, *Germania* (Oxford University translation)

*Tacitus* was a Roman historian who never stepped foot on Germanic soil. As a sincere student of historical and government records, he artfully cobbled together many older and contemporary works in the creation of his *De Origine et situ Germanorum* (commonly referred to as *Germania*). Because his was not a first-hand account, the initial challenge that arises in the above chapter deals with the various translations of the name 'Hertha': *Ertha, Ertham, Hertham, Herthum, Necthum, Nertum, Nerthus,* and *Verthum*. There exists no original copy of *Germania* and all copies of this text date to the late 15th and early 16th century, and are based on a Roman document from approximate 1426 CE – also now lost.

**Part Two: Terra Mater**

Overwhelmingly, all scholars agree on 'Terra Mater' (*..nisi quod in commune Herthum, id est Terram matrem*); everything else – from identity to function – is up for interpretation. This perhaps explains why so many books and papers have been written on the subject of Terra Mater in this particular reference, even relating the wagon to the Hebrew *Ark of the Covenant* (1). Apparently, the force of this mysterious Terra Mater is such that, though none can agree wholly on her gender, manner or location of worship, this Germanic fertility goddess (according to Tacitus) has come to reside deep within our subconscious mind; namely, that great wellspring which offers us reflections dimly sensed and distantly experienced.

The first examination of this subject begins in the name *Nerthus*, which Rudolf Simek, the Germanist and philologist, relates "*is exactly the same form of the name which would correspond to the ON god Njordr.*" (2). Based on this statement, the topic of Nerthus changes from identity and function to that of gender; namely: is she a consort to *Njord*, is she actually a *he*, or is she/he a hermaphrodite?

*Njord* is considered the Old Norse linguistic equivalent of Nerthus, meaning some scholars have determined that either he always was a male, or was a female who become male; an idea not that far-fetched, nor the idea of shared masculine-feminine characteristics, when the linguistics for this argument are examined. For the most part, all the points above can be examined by a closer inspection of the Indo-European root word *ner-,* which has two definitions (3). The first, *\*ner-1*, means, "under; north", and is seen in Old English "north; northern", Middle Dutch *nort*, meaning "north" (also *Norman* and *Norwegian*), and Old Norse *nordhr*, or "north". The next definition, *\*ner-2*, means, "man; vigorous, vital, strong", and its root stems from *\*e₂ner-*, meaning, *andro-*, which is Greek for "man", as in andro (man) + gene (woman) = androgynous; and -*andry*, also Greek, meaning "having a number of husbands", as in polyandry. Then, from Old and Modern German, *ner* means, "turning, winding; refuge, safety, asylum". Overall, these theories have two challenges: first, making the linguistic leap from *ner* to *nj* (from Germanic to Greek); and second, determining if the Germanic tribes venerated a singular/chief female deity.

Considering the other names: *Herthum*, *Hertham*, *Ertham*, and *Ertha* (and to some extent *Njord*), all of these can be linked back to Modern German *erde*, meaning, "earth". The Indo-European root for "earth, ground" is *\*ert-*, as seen in Old English *eorthe*, Middle English *erthe*, and Middle Dutch *aerde*, *eerde*, all meaning, "earth". The Greek root for this is *khthōn*, meaning, "earth"; this is also where the word *chthonic* comes from, which "pertains to deities, spirits, and other beings dwelling under the earth." The Indo-European root for this is *dhghem-*, meaning "earthling", as seen in Old Norse *gumi* and Old English *guma*, both meaning, "groom; man". Other words that share this root are: humility, humus, in- and exhume, homo-, and homicide. Returning to the Greek aspect, *khthōn*, this word is found in two other Terra Maters: *Kolyo* and *Calypso*.

Kolyo is a Proto-Indo-European word meaning, "the coverer", and she is the goddess of death – more than an overseer of the realm of death, Kolyo is death personified, and her favored implement is the noose (4). Calypso is a Greek nymph, specifically a *naiad*, and her name means, "to conceal; to hide". Regarding naiads, the word means "to flow", and signifies brooks that spring from wells; overall, they are prophetic beings and healers, and though generally benevolent, are brutally dangerous to humans who hurt or damage their territory. Both these names are found in Indo-European *kel-*, meaning, "to cover, conceal, save", and is seen in Old English *hell* and *heall* ("hall"); Old Norse *Hel* (realm and goddess of the dead); and Germanic *\*haljo*, meaning "the underworld". Other words that share this root are: hole, Valhalla, sheath, hold, hull and husk, helm, cellar, and conceal.

Another name to be considered is *Ing*, which can be noted with some frequency:
-An ancestor of the *Ingaevones*, a North Sea Germanic tribe.
-A Rune in both the Germanic and Anglo-Saxon Futhark, and deserving of a direct passage in the *Anglo-Saxon Rune Poem* (*Ingwar*).
-A name for King Hroðgar in *Beowulf* 1319 (*frea Ingwina*, "lord of Ing's friends").
-The *Ynglings*, the (past and current) Swedish royal dynasty; and the mythological sons of *Mannus*.

-*Yngvi*, an additional name for Freyr, as in *Yngvi-Freyr*.
-Possibly, Gothic *iggws / yggr*, "anxious".
-The Old Norse, Anglo-Saxon, and Provincial English word *ing*, meaning "meadow, pasture; a low lying area near a river" (reference Danish *eng*, and Swedish *äng* – as in Angles, the tribe).
-And a commonplace Old Danish, Old Swedish, Old West Norse element found in modern personal names (5).

This extensive etymology is necessary in that *Pliny* mentions the *Ingvaeones* as one of five Germanic tribes, and Tacitus lists them as one of three who live "near the ocean"; both of these claims are supported by archeology. Combined, this information gives strength to the idea of Ingui as the first king of Sweden, the father of Njord, and grandfather of Freyr (*Historia Norwegiae*); which is similar to Sturluson's claim from the *Poetic Edda* that Odinn's son Yngvi reigned in Sweden. So from this, it appears that before Odinn/Wodan became the dominating force in the Germanic pantheon, Ingui was the ancient ancestral god of the Angles ('Ingles') within continental Germania. Further, in support of this claim, he had a wagon. From the *Anglo-Saxon Rune Poem* (Wright translation):

> Ing wæs ærest mid East-Denum
> gesewen secgun, oþ he siððan est
> ofer wæg gewat; wæn æfter ran;
> ðus Heardingas ðone hæle nemdun.


> Ing was first among the East-Danes,
> seen by men. Then he went eastwards
> across the sea, The wagon sped after,
> thus the Heardings have named the hero.

This passage is certainly suggestive of Nerthus' wagon, so that, if Nerthus was male and the wagon procession was part of his worship – perhaps even including *Gunnars Thattr helmings* from *Flaeyjarbok*, into this scenario (where a statue of Freyr travels the countryside with a priestess) – then Tacitus' account could be an example of him applying Roman religious practices to little understood Germanic cultural tradition. In that *Germania* was written in the first century and the *Anglo-Saxon Rune Poem* in the 12th century, this may be yet another reason for Ing's long-enduring mythology (as part of folk-memory).

Returning to the name Njord, according to Heathen Lore he is one of the *Vanir*, father to *Freyr* and *Freyja*, and is strongly associated with the sea and seafaring; this latter being something he shares with his son Freyr. Ships and seafaring are an indelible aspect of Bronze Age rock carvings, so certainly a prominent thought within the minds of the tribes of that era, lending proof to both the importance of Njord and his connections to open water. *Skáldskaparmál* relates an interesting story about Njord and Skadi – how she chooses him based solely on the appearance of his feet. According to Greek Mythology, the feet are symbols of the soul; an assertion made by Diel when he highlights the lameness of *Dionysus*, *Hephaestus*, *Wayland the Blacksmith*, and *Mani*, who all had deformed feet and blemished souls (6). Certainly Heathen lore makes reference to this area as one of vulnerability, as was the case with Baldr, Hroi (from *Reykdœla saga og Víga-Skútu*), and from Welsh myth, Lleu Llaw Gyffes. As to Skadi, she is a *Gýgjar*, a female giant and Wisdom-Keeper, a goddess of hunting and skiing, but her marriage to Njord fails because she longs to hunt in the snow-covered mountains, running with wolves (a character trait of Seiðwomen), and he longs to reside in *Noatun*, or 'ship-town', by the sea. Conclusively, Njord can be related to ships and sea travel; suggestively, perhaps he was invoked in ship burials, like those found at Sutton Hoo, near Woodbridge, England (6th century CE); the Ladbyskibet ship burial in Denmark, on the island of Fyn (900 CE); the Storhaug ship burial in Stavanger, Norway (690 – 750 CE); or the Oseberg ship burial near Tønsberg, Norway (820 CE) (to cite a few examples). Otherwise, there is no evidence of Njord in personal or place names on the Germanic continent; they are, however, found with regularity in Scandinavia. This indicates that Nerthus worship among the Germanic tribes could not have included the name 'Njord'.

When considering the Vanir and their known gods – Njord, Freyr, and Freyja – we must also examine their function. Primarily, they are fertility gods who are called upon to bring about a good harvest, a fair wind, plentiful rain, and an abundant catch from the sea. Most scholars equate the fertility figures depicted on Bronze Age rock carvings as representations of the Vanir. Suggestively, Ing and Ullr belong on this list, but the inclusion of either is not certain. This is important to remember because nowhere in *Germania* does Tacitus relate the name of a <u>known</u> Northern Germanic deity; instead he uses what he considers to be their Roman equivalents: *Hercules* and *Isis*, *Mars*, *Mercury*, and *Oceanus*. If Nerthus worship were as important as indicated, then, reasonably, there would remain towns, rivers, and mountains, even personal names that have maintained a semblance of this name. There simply are no such remnants on the Germanic continent.

"Terram matrem" is how Tacitus described her, a name that translates as 'earth mother'. The Roman equivalent of this idea is found in several other names; such as *Ceres*, *Cybele*, *Rhea*, and *Tellus*, so that each will be examined.

-Ceres is the goddess of cultivated plants (particularly cereals) and maternal love. Her name is rooted in Indo-European *ker-* and means, "to grow"; other words related to this root include cereal, create, crescent, accrue, and increase. Her Greek equivalent is *Demeter*, and her festival was held in May.

-Cybele is a 6th century Phrygian earth goddess, a deity of life, death and rebirth; she is the personification of caves and mountains, wild places and beasts. She was worshipped in ancient Anatolia from Neolithic times. The Romans referred to her as *potnia theron*, which alludes to her Neolithic root as "Mistress of Animals"; also, *Magna Mater*, meaning, 'Great Mother" and *Mater Idaea*, referring to Mount Ida, "Goose Mountain", the supposed place of her birth in northwest Turkey. Burkert suggests that Mater refers to 'foreign gods', and that this word is not found in the Phrygian language, but is of Luwian origin (7). Of note, the Anatolians were the earliest Indo-European speaking tribes, whose languages were Hittite, Luwian, and Palaic. It is from Luwian that we find the oldest reference to *Tyr*, as *tiwar(z)* in their language, and meaning, "sun, day; shining being" (8).

According to myth, Cybele initiated Dionysus (one of the lame gods mentioned above), and his cult is said to resemble hers. Also from myth, Cybele was either: raped by Zeus, or sprung up from his spilt sperm where it landed upon a stone, the result of either was said to be *Agdistis*, a hermaphrodite *daemon*, or a dual-sexed deity of fate and fortune (daemons are also personal attendant spirits). By nature, Agdistis is wild, powerfully creative, fully aware, and dispenses life or death at will. Frightened, the Greek gods had Dionysus get her/him drunk by turning the water that gushes from a spring into wine; once drunk her/his genitals were bound in such a way that when s/he was startled awake, they were ripped off. Where they landed, an almond tree grew – alongside the spring – and Cybele, fully a woman now, was 'born'. In a rock-cut Phrygian monument to Cybele, she is depicted wearing a long belted dress, a high cylindrical hat, and a veil that covers her body (See *Part Five: Keeping Time*). Her worship spread from the mountains to the coast, and she is often depicted holding a small vase while sitting within a wagon drawn by lions with birds of prey flying overhead. As an aside, Cybele had a son named *Attis* who was also her lover. Driven mad by her, he castrated himself; thereafter he was the attendant of her lion-driven wagon. Upon his death, he was reborn as an evergreen tree.

-Tellus (also Terra) is Rome's most ancient of goddess', dating to 268 BCE. She is the protectress of cultivated farmland, marriage and pregnancy (in women and animals); one of her symbols is the seed, denoting every stage of growth, from planting to harvest. So important are her gifts of fertility and growth, that she has three festival days: *Paganalia* in February (a sowing festival); *Fordicalia* in April, where cows are sacrificed, their fetuses burnt, their ashes used to bless crops; and *Feriae Sementivae* in December (a harvesting festival). Tellus and Ceres are closely linked and they both are honored during Paganalia (Tellus during the first part in late January, and Ceres in the last part, the first of February). They are often mentioned together, as in this poem by Ovid (*Fasti* I:24):

> *O Mothers of Fruitfulness, Tellus and Ceres /*
> *with salted spelt cakes offered to you / in kind service /*
> *Tellus and Ceres /*
> *you who gave grain life / gave us room to grow. /*

*May You grant tender seed abundant increase.*
*Let not icy cold enwrap our new shoots with snow,*
*while we sow let cloudless skies and fair winds blow.*
*When the seed lies sprouting, sprinkle with gentle rains,*
*may you ward off the feasting by birds from our grains. /*
*Meanwhile may our grain not blight by rough mildew,*
*nor foul weather our seed blanch to a sickly hue. /*
*Look now, Good Mothers, guard well the field,*
*the seasons change, the earth by your breath grows warm,*
*with your gentle touch may you increase our yield.*

-Rhea was a Titaness, or female Titan (giant; Gygjar), who married her brother Cronus, and together they ruled as King and Queen of the Gods (until dethroned by Zeus, their son). So that her husband would not kill her sixth child Zeus (as he had done all the previous children), she hid him away on Mount Id (birthplace of Cybele). So close in identity are Rhea and Cybele that the Greeks contended that the two were the same; specifically, that Rhea had left Crete to escape Cronus, fleeing to the wild mountains of northwest Turkey (Asia Minor. Seiðwomen seem to have a penchant for wild places). She is often depicted sitting within a wagon drawn by two lions; likewise, the swan is associated with her. Other goddesses, such as the Sumerian *Gula*, *Tanit* in Cartage, the *Lady with Snakes* in Crete, *Artemis* in Greece, and *Anahita* in Anatolia, can all be associated with processions, wagons, and human sacrifice.

Finally, returning to the other translations of Nerthus, namely: Herthum, Hertham, Ertham, and Ertha, again, all of these are firmly rooted in "earth", and still seen in Modern German *erde*, "earth". Beatus Rhenanus, a German humanist, religious reformer and classical scholar, was the first to render Nerthus into 'Herthum' in 1519. According to Motz this has been a debatable association, even though the "syllable *hert, hart* is quite productive in west Germanic speech" (9). She goes on to mention several place names, such as *Herthen, Hertenstein,* and *Hertford,* and the personal names *Hartvinc, Gerhard,* and *Hertha.* This last relating to a "supposed Germanic 'earth-mother'", per Simek, based on a misreading of the name Nerthus. Clearly, and beyond doubt, the speculation surrounding this subject began at the first translation of *Germania* and continues today, so that every possible point has been examined, outlined, and reviewed by untold scholars, with little agreement amongst them. So it is, at this juncture, that an exploration of the *activities* around this mysterious entity will be examined.

In an essay entitled: *The Goddess Nerthus: A New Approach*, Motz makes an impressive argument for Nerthus having survived throughout Germany as *Frau Holle* and *Perchte* – both early Germanic winter goddesses. Regarding this theory, Davidson notes, *"..this hardly seems to be borne out by the evidence Waschnitius collected, and spinning is not confined to winter. However, they certainly visited homes at Christmas,.."* Indeed, Frau Holda is a winter goddess with a varied function: spinning and other domestic duties, childbirth, domestic animals, Seiðcraft, and the Wild Hunt. Likewise, Perchta too is a winter goddess who is said to visit homes during Twelfth Night. Concerned with domestic affairs, she assures that both children and servants perform their household tasks, and is particularly concerned with spinning productivity. Of the two, Frau Holda's name has taken on many forms, such as *Hulda, Holle, Hilde,* and *Hel*; this latter is based on Holle/Hölle, which is the German word for "hell". More than any other time of year, Frau Holda and Perchta are associated with Yule and the Wild Hunt. Additionally, they:
-are considered household goddesses of spinning,
-dole out punishment and/or reward, particularly in regard to young girls and women,
-are capable of appearing either young/lovely or old/hideous,

-are associated with dogs/wolves and goats (the *Julbok* or Yule Goat is linked to them),
-are more prone to flying than walking from one place to another,
-they dwell in the wild, and
-are associated with wild places. Finally, Frau Holda's name may be akin to *huldra*, the 'hidden folk' of Norwegian folk tradition; a name that means "covered; secret". Huldra are rulers or guardians of wild places, are both male and female, directly interact with humans – during no specific time of year – and can appear as either beautiful or ugly. From this, it appears that Frau Holda is more akin to the 'hidden folk' of lore than a seasonal goddess; albeit, one so revered that warriors lay down their weapons in her presence. Combining her known characteristics it seems appropriate to honor her on Mother's Night.

## Part Three: Eleven Observations

Aside from the name 'Nerthus', *Germania*'s chapter 40 makes eleven observations, which have been categorized below to better explore them.

1-Seven tribes unite to worship Terra Mater.

--Each of the seven tribes is said to worship Nerthus; they are the Langobardi, Reudigni, Avions, Angli, Varini, Eudoses, Suardones, and Nuithones.

---The Langobardi are the Lombards or "Long Beards", from *Origo Gentis Langobardorum*, a 7th century text detailing their origins and exploits. From the beginning of this tale, their ruler was a woman named *Gambara* who prayed to Frigg for victory (their enemy prayed to Wodan). Frigg advised their women to bind their long hair beneath their chin, and join their men in battle. When Wodan awoke, he promised to bless the first tribe he saw, which, due to Frigg's council, was the soon to be named Langobardi tribe; for upon first seeing them he exclaimed, "Who are those Longbeards?" Their region extended from Bavaria in the south to northern Germania along the Elbe River. From the account of their name, it is reasonable to assume that the ruler Gambara led her people in worship of the goddess Frigg.

---The Reudigni origins and identity are unknown; their name, however, is thought to be found in Randers and Randsfjord, Denmark.

---The Avions / Auiones name means "island people" and are thought to have lived on Öland Island off the coast of Småland in southern Sweden.

---The Angles lived in the area of modern day Schleswig, Germany, and are thought to have originated there, along the Baltic, mostly upon the Jutland peninsula.

---The Varni / Varini / Varinnae / Waerne name means 'defenders' and are thought to have originated in southern Scandinavia but migrated to northern Germania, in the modern day area of Mecklenburg. In Scandinavia they are said to have resided alongside the Geats.

---The Jutes are thought to have given their name to Jutland, and lived along the Frisian coast.

---The Suarines are thought to have left their name in the modern day northern German town of Schwerin.

---The Nuithones are thought to be the Teutones or Euthiones. If so, their name may be akin to Njord or Noatin,

2-These tribes agree that Terra Mater has a direct role in their affairs; and that Terra Mater visits every tribe.

--These seven tribes, according to Tacitus, agreed that Nerthus' influence was such that s/he had direct interaction. This implies, to 'walk among', or to 'dwell among', or to 'directly interact with'. This sort of relationship – between god and man – is rarely heard of in Heathen lore. For example, if the above statement can be taken as true, then Nerthus is awake and aware of herself and her surroundings, actively engaging in a direct relationship with her folk. Certainly this indicates an entity with a soul; a condition quite unlike a Christian god who communicates only via designated priests, or a Hindu and/or Buddhist god that is worshipped through a *murti* (stature or divine form). In this account, Nerthus appears to be a living embodiment that walks among the folk of seven tribes. As such, she would be nothing less than a tribal entity, a mother figure for all folk. (An example may perhaps be drawn here with *Veleda*, a Bructeri priestess and Seiðwoman, who is mentioned during the Batavian Rebellion, by Gaius Julius Civilis, as having been a spiritual leader of her people, and having rightly predicted the outcome of her Germanic tribe against the Roman legions – 70 ACE.)

3-Upon an "island of the ocean" there is a sacred grove that contains a holy wagon, covered with a veil, and attended only by a priest.

--Several possible locations have been suggested for this island; some of them include:

---*Als*, off the east coast of Jutland; one of its cities is named Nordborg. Als is the site of the Hjortspring boat find from the pre-Roman Iron Age. It is a 13-meter long wood boat capable of holding a crew of 23 men that appears to have been purposely sunk as a war sacrifice. When excavated, the boat contained 131 Celtic-type shields and 33 artfully crafted shield bosses, 10 iron swords, 138 iron spearheads, and one mail coat.

---*Borremose Fort*, a pre-Roman Iron Age settlement in North Jutland. The fortress is a raised earth platform located within a bog and has an inner moat. It contained several long houses, cobbled roads, and the surrounding bogs contained several sacrificial bodies, clothing, and weaponry.

---*Fyn / Funen*, Denmark's third largest island; its capital city is Odense. The island is famous for, among other things, being the site of the Ladbyskibet ship burial.

---*Heligoland*, a German archipelago in the North Sea, its original name was Heyligeland, or "holy land". This island is commonly considered the one mentioned by Tacitus as a location sacred to the Angli, where they held sacred rites. Commonly, it is associated with *Forseti*, whose name means "fore-seated; first-seated". Forseti is god of the Thing, of justice and truth. His home is *Glitnir*, which means, "shining", and is said to have a silver ceiling and golden pillars that radiate light, making it visible from a distance. Heligoland has a 50 meter white cliff and several free standing red sandstone pillars that rise out of the shore some 47 meters. According to Heathen lore, Forseti collected the laws from every tribe, embarked upon a sea voyage to a remote island, and there he compiled them into a workable format. Forseti's island has a holy spring and became such a sacred place that no one dared raid or commit violence there, for fear of punishment. Traditionally, all major legal assemblies were held here, and all disputes dealt with only during daylight hours and never in winter, for it was believed that darkness was the opposite of truth and resolution of conflict. Otherwise, trees do not grow well on Heligoland due to the high winds; therefore, there are no 'sacred groves'. Nor is there any lake.

(Heligoland used to be one island, until a flood in 1720 CE separated it into two.)

---*Hiddensee*, off the coast of Germany is a long and narrow island that could accommodate a single-track roadway for a wagon.

---*Lejre*, a town on the island of Zealand in Denmark; its Old Norse name was *Hleiðra*. Many scholars have attempted to find *Heorot Hall* here (mentioned in *Beowulf*). Whether this is true or not, the German chronicler Thietmar of Merseburg, in 1015 CE, provided the following account from the German Emperor Henry I, from 934 CE:

*"I have heard strange stories about their sacrificial victims in ancient times, and I will not allow the practice to go unmentioned. In one place called Lederun (Lejre), the capital of the realm in the district of Selon (Sjælland), all the people gathered every nine years in January, that is after we have celebrated the birth of the Lord, and there they offered to the gods ninety-nine men and just as many horses, along with dogs and hawks."*

---*Rügen*, off the coast of Germany, with a lake called *Herthasee*; however, most of the archeological remains found here are Slavic, not Germanic. Rügen was said to be home to *Svantovit*, a Slavic god of war, divination, and protector of the fields, who, according to Saxo Grammaticus (written circa 1200 CE), resided in a temple there surrounded by a Rowan grove. Svantovit, whose name means *World Seer*, is said to have four faces, was draped in purple robes, and 'great treasure' was sacrificed to him. The priest of Svantovit would prepare special honey cakes and feed this to his image with ale during the regular spring and harvest festivals. Svantovit was said to ride a white horse at night, bringing terror/nightmares to tribal enemies. His priests determined omens from a white horse kept in the temple (1).

---Finally, there is a possibility that this 'island' is underwater, based on recent discoveries (2).


4-The priest of Terra Mater becomes aware of her existence "in" the wagon, and so begins the procession that will visit every tribe (becomes aware of terrestrial and celestial events?).

--This could refer to someone who is aware of terrestrial and possibly celestial events such as seasonal changes, or the occurrence of constellations. (See *Part Five: Keeping Time*)

5-During this "season" everyone is happy and there is great festivity; no conflict or war is allowed during this time, no weapons are raised against another.

---This indicates a festival, generally of the seasonal variety, perhaps even a law assembly. (In the Battle of Thermopylae in 480 BCE, for example, the '300' Spartans did not receive support from their fellow Greeks due to most of them competing in the Olympics, which restricted them from bearing arms in combat.)

6-That Terra Mater visits every tribe.

--Considering that all seven tribes lived in northern Germany, Jutland, and Denmark, this is feasible. As such, it further suggests a central meeting place, perhaps an island, as mentioned by Tacitus. Likewise, because the priests were aware of her presence, they were responsible/relied upon to herald the beginning and end of the festivities. Another consideration is a college/learning center of priests with centralized knowledge, then this celebration could have taken place in several locations at the same time.

7-Cattle draw Terra Mater's wagon.

--Several highly decorative wagons have been found in bogs. Aside from being a regular means of transportation, wagons are often found in burial mounds, with the owner laid upon it with all their possessions and finery.

8-The priest returns Terra Mater to her temple at a designated time.

--The priest is the determining factor; s/he signals both the beginning and end of festivities. Further, it was a standard custom to 'mark' or otherwise bless an area by carrying a figure or burning torch about the circumference; or perhaps the wagon itself was sacred, conveying blessings to the seven tribes. (See *Part Five: Keeping Time*)

9-Upon returning to the temple, Terra Mater, and the curtain that concealed her from open view, is washed in a "secret lake".

--Washing religious statues and their clothing is standard in Indo-European practices, and something still seen today at Hindu temples (reference: *murti*).

10-Slaves perform the washing of Terra Mater, and the veil; they are then 'swallowed up'.
--Specifically, the passage reads the "lake instantly swallows up", therefore being under water, suggesting ritual drowning.

11-Anyone who looks directly upon Terra Mater (the slaves) must die.
--This begs to question:  Did the priest look upon her?  If so, and they kept their lives, perhaps it was their service to Terra Mater that spared their lives; meaning, they lived to serve.  Then, another way of reading this is, 'those who are about to die are granted a look at Terra Mater'.  In modern-day terms this could translate as 'unswerving devotion'.

From these eleven observations, some bare 'facts' do emerge:
-The Langobards called upon Frigg for favors (Gambara, their female ruler, and a female divinity at the head of a pantheon; an All-Mother).
-The area of the seven tribes extends from Jutland in the west to the Oder River in the east.
-These tribes believe Terra Mater to play a key role in their daily lives.
-Worship was carried out on an "island of the ocean".
-A priest or possible group of priests – college/learning center – heralded the beginning and end of festivities.
-The wagon was large enough to be drawn by cattle.
-This worship involved festivities and a cessation of conflict.
-At the end of festivities, Terra Mater's image and coverings are ceremoniously washed.
-Slaves do the washing of the image and covering, afterwards, they are given as sacrifice.

Undoubtedly, the Celtic and Germanic tribes practiced human sacrifice – a practice carried out since Neolithic times.  The Celts, for example, would build large wicker figures, fill them with humans and animals, and then burn the entire structure.  Likewise, prisoners of war were sacrificed as offerings to Celtic gods, presumably as a means of thanksgiving for victory in combat.  Nor was there one specific means of sacrifice, but several.  Such as:
-sacrifices to *Esus* were hanged;

-those given to *Teutates* were drowned; and

-*Taranis'* sacrifices were immolated.

Notable in this consideration is that Wodan sacrificed 'his self to his Self', hanging upon a tree (was Wodan's god Esus? And what of Kolyo, the Goddess of Death, whose favored implement was the noose?). According to Tacitus, Saxo, and Adam von Bremen, sacrifice was an integral aspect of Germanic life. Warriors would go to their graves with their slaves, wives would sacrifice themselves to join their husbands, temples were the places of mass human sacrifices (until the 11<sup>th</sup> century according to Adam von Bremen), and *Ynglinga saga* mentions the sacrifice of kings and the sons of kings. And if Ibn Fadlan's account can be believed, there was a woman, the 'Angel of Death', who assured that such sacrifices were carried out properly. Considering that Teutates – whose name means 'tribe', 'father of the tribe' or 'tribal protector' – accepts sacrifices who have been drowned. Perhaps a correlation can be made using Motz's assertion that the 'terra' in Terra Mater denotes a non-Roman, tribal entity. If this is the case, it is tempting to see Frigg as not just the tribal goddess of the 'Long Beards', but of the other six tribes as well. However, because there is no known reference to Frigg demanding human sacrifice, there can be no clear connection made between her and the sacrifices to Nerthus in this instance.

**Part Four:  Human Sacrifice**

Over one thousand bodies have been found in bogs; most met their mortal end through remarkable violence. Though bog bodies date from 8,000 BCE to a few centuries before our own, most are found in Northern Germania, Britain, and Ireland. Some of these bodies are so well preserved that they appear to be 'sleeping'; or, such was the condition of their body upon discovery that the police, in some cases, were called in to investigate a homicide. Other bodies are not so well preserved, being nothing more than a fractured skull and arm or leg bones that have been hacked off. Nor is there any particular gender or age group to be found among them; apparently, men, women, children, old, middle-age, and young all were seemingly given (volunteered?) as sacrifices. If there is a common theme it seems to be that they were all wealthy to middle-class, well-groomed, well dressed, comparatively healthy, and mostly fed a diet of grain prior to death.

Nor was this a regular means of disposing of bodies after death. Although the period in which bog bodies have been found is one that lasted several hundred years, the regular means of internment before, during, and after this age is either cremation or mound burial. Even so, sacrifices – human or otherwise – were such a frequent occurrence that they are mentioned casually in *Hyndluljoth*, where Freyja's *Hörgr* is "reddened with blood" and "fused like glass" from the fires kindled there. Perhaps a body in a bog was a <u>complete</u> body, unlike one cremated and placed in an urn, for a specific reason. Conjecturally, the reason could be that the god being sacrificed to needed a whole body, one that had met its end via a sacred means, rather than a pile of ash and bone. If so, to what end would a seemingly be-souled god – like Nerthus, who walks among the tribes – have for a whole bodied 'servant'? Certainly there exists an element long forgotten in the folk memory of such practices – such as the need for human sacrifice in the first place.

It has been suggested that human sacrifice – based on the many cultures that practiced this form of worship – was a necessary exchange of life in return for godly aid or a greater common cause. Offering an entire body as sacrifice, this act could well represent the whole passing from one form of existence into the next, from Midgard to Asgard, so to speak. Assuredly, the Old European ancestors viewed death as a form of existence akin to life; so could not sacrifice then be a means of 'transportation' from one realm to the next? An intriguing example of a human sacrifice/initiation is found on *Inner Plate E* of the Gundestrup Cauldron (an object found in a bog and thought to be given as a sacrifice). This particular panel is divided into an above and below section. Below, there is a line of warriors with plain cap/helmets, spears and shields moving towards a figure three times larger than all others, who is 'ritually drowning' a soldier (according to most interpretations); there is a rampant dog/wolf at the larger figure's feet, facing the soldiers. Following the bottom panel soldiers with shields, is a single soldier who carries only a sword and is wearing a boar-crested helmet, and behind him are three lure players. This lower scene is separated from the upper by a blooming/flowering branch. In the upper scene there are four riders on horses, moving away from the drowning scene, each of them is wearing an ornate helmet; seemingly leading their way is a serpent.

Suggestively, the bottom panel soldiers could be undergoing a ritual drowning; a process that J. P. Mallory describes as, *"a ceremonial drowning scene, the classic method of dispatching a victim to a 'third function' fertility deity in Western Europe."* If so, then this could be similar to accounts of slaves who were sent into battle with only a sword, their survival being the means by which they gained entrance into the warband; meaning, they became part of the Dumézilian Trifunctional Hypothesis – moving from the lowest class to that of the highest. Mallory further asserts how the ancient Gauls *"made offerings to three gods – Esus, Taranis and Teutates – by recourse of hanging, burning and drowning, respectively; and how this pattern was also found in the Germanic manner of punishment, via hanging, stabbing, and drowning."* A fact easily supported in light of the multiple means of 'death' brought upon the bog bodies, who often received all three forms of punishment. Another suggestion for this practice is offered by Kris Kershaw who suggests this scene to be a *"pagan baptism"* where a youth, who has been training to be a warrior, or full member of the tribe, is ritually put to death via immersion, then 'reborn' as a man or full member of the folk (1). In both examples given, death by drowning was a means to bring about fertility; or as the great Hindu sage Yogatrayananda wrote, *"Any action which may promote the betterment of man has of necessity the nature of a ritual sacrifice."* (2) As I detail in the *Introduction*, it is partially upon this idea that I have researched this subject: to outline, explain, and possibly re-create a meaningful ritual process by which folk may come into Heathenry, or may connect/reconnect with Heathenry, or may dedicate self to Self (a personal god), or prove themselves worthy by serving their kinsmen through individual sacrifice.

Death by drowning, or being placed in a bog, must be a means to directly communicate with a tutelary spirit – a guardian and protector of the tribe. Today, throughout Europe, in the areas being discussed, river and lake spirits abound, and come complete with tales of their eagerness to lure victims to a murky death. The Poles know them as *wilas*, the Greeks as *harpies* and *naiads*, the Indo-Europeans as *nagas*, the Celts as *merrows*, and the English as *mermaids*. Then in Wales there is the war goddess *Aerfen* who presides over the outcome of battle, and demands three human sacrifices every year (3). Interestingly enough, it is said even today – in England, Wales, Scandinavia and Denmark – that if someone does *not* drown then a voice is heard from the water that says, *"The hour is come but the man is not."* (3a). According to English folk tradition that hour is St. Valentine's eve, which traditionally was after the first full moon after Yule (according to the pre-Christian calendar). As such, the time of year for a drowning appears to coincide with *Disting* and *Disablot* – both particular to female divine beings.

Returning to Tacitus, he relates that the drowned victims were slaves, yet the bog bodies appear to be nobly born individuals with 'soft' hands and unbroken bones, well dressed with manicured nails, so seemingly not accustomed to the hard labor of slaves. Nor are bodies the only sacrifice. Well-crafted swords and spears, shields and ornately carved wagons, the magnificent Gundestrup Cauldron, and other remarkable treasures have been found in bogs; and as Hutton points out, *"The wealth which they represent is apparently more than could have been dedicated by local rulers"*; and, *"It's also a tremendous symbol of rebirth, just as food can be transformed in it, so a human soul can be transformed. It's a symbol of death and drowning, a symbol of fire, because a blaze is beneath it."* (4). This suggests, again, something more than a slave or the possessions of a slave, but objects and persons of value to the tribe – to several tribes.

Within the Republic of India, sacrifice remains a regular practice; as it has for thousands of years. In all, India today is a land were paganism has never been suppressed, a land were even today blood sacrifices are carried out in accord to ancient Vedic traditions. The core philosophy behind these practices is the nature of creation, which is the nature of the universe. A common expression in India today is, *"To live is to devour life"*, and this 'devouring' is seen as the only permanent reality, even an entity who is seen as so powerful that it is only through alliance with it that human progress has been made. This entity in India – this all-powerful, all-consuming being – is Agni, which is fire personified, and he must be fed. *Chandogya Upanisad* 3:6:3 relates, *"Actually, the gods do not eat nor do they drink, but seeing the offering they are pleased"*; and in the *Taittiriya*

*Upanisad* 2:2:1, "*All creatures are born from food; whatever dwells on the earth lives by food and shall turn into food in the end.*" Certainly, from the many references given throughout this essay, it can be seen that a sacrifice must be in accord to the nature and purpose of tribe – that a god must be placated, a place of offering established, and the offering itself be of worth.

In that drowning appears to be the means by which the condition of fertility is either created or maintained, and that fertility would have been the most basic need in the daily search of food, shelter, safety and livelihood, it is essentially confirmed as the best means to bring about that result. After all, if there were no food available, then the entire tribe would suffer, or they would be forced to become slaves. No doubt, a poor harvest followed by a long winter could mean starvation for entire villages, a situation that calls for preventative measures – such is the need of varied manual and technical skills coupled with assistance from a divine source. Which could be why drowning was such an attractive option, for it could represent the exact moment when that which is offered passes <u>immediately</u> to its divine destination. And if so, this would further imply that the victim had to be made holy, perhaps by receiving the 'marks' of the gods themselves, such as hanging and stabbing. After all, the life so given would assure the very continuity of tribe. Further, and importantly, the victim had to be willing. In fact, the holiness of the sacrifice would depend on this. As unwelcome as this idea may sound to modern ears, our ancient ancestors may have realized a unique relationship between themselves and their environment – a divinely inspired gifting cycle – one more directly relatable between themselves and their gods, between themselves and the sacrificing priests, and so went to this fate willingly. Old European lore relates how men and women volunteered to die and so "join" a husband or chieftain onto the next life; and there are accounts of animal sacrifices that were well fed and well cared for prior to their being sacrificed. In this latter, it was believed that when the animal 'met god' and related its miss-treatment, the god would punish the tribe. Because a sacrifice must meet the demands of the need, could not a human life be the one sacrifice to assure the promise of all other life?

According to Tacitus there was a specific time for these events to take place, that a priest (possibly group of priests, in different locations, based on terrestrial and celestial observation) would signal the beginning and end of Nerthus' appearance. One way of determining a possible time is by examining the stomach contents of the bog bodies. Mostly, stomach contents have revealed that the victims' last meal consisted of grains, possibly a porridge. From this, scientists have concluded that since no fruits, vegetables or meat have been found in the stomachs of bog bodies, then their last meal was standard wintertime fare (5). Plant specialists have determined that this winter porridge was mostly a mix of wild, uncultivated seeds, such as camelina (45% omega-3 fatty acids), spergula (a wild flower), knotgrass (weed seed), barley, and flax (these last two being cultivated plants). In all, 40 different types of seed have been identified in some bog bodies. In that a few of these seeds where probably cultivated, others may have been added as filler; but no cereal grains have been found. Even so, this meal should not be considered the poor meal of a lowly sacrifice, for according to the *Æcerbot Galdr* – an 11th century Anglo-Saxon charm meant as a "field remedy" – seed and grain are a life-giving blessing:

*Erce, Erce, Erce, Earth Mother..grant us..*
*fields growing and thriving..*
*bright shafts of millet crops, and broad barley crops,*
*and white wheat crops, and all the crops of the earth. /*
*Fields filled with food for the use of man. /*
*grant us growing gifts and prove each grain of use.*

If human sacrifices were carried out at the end of winter to assure spring fertility and the renewal of tribal life, how was the date determined? According to Tacitus' account the Nerthus rites were carried out at a specific time of year by a priest. Aside from officiating at sacrifices (later, this role further included Germanic judicial matters), priests may have also been *Time Keepers*.

**Part Five: Keeping Time**
From the existing lore it would seem that the Germanic tribes recognized five periods/seasons of the year, all based on the full moon: Winter Night in October; Yule in December; Disting in March; Summer Finding in June; and, Harvest in August. Though each has import, seemingly Disting was the highlight of the year in that it was both an annual market and Thing (this latter being a law assembly where matters were discussed and settled between the

many tribal leaders). But how were these dates determined? How would so many tribes, spread over a large area of land, know when to converge? Certainly, there had to be Time Keepers. The Bronze Age (1600 BCE) Nebra Sky Disc has been speculated to be a means of time keeping; and if found authentic, will *re*-confirm the already existing megaliths that serve as astronomical time-pieces. Otherwise, there are the Runic or 'perpetual' calendars which are based on the Metonic Cycle, a 19 year lunar calendar (1). However, because the earliest known Runic Calendars come from the 13th century, it is uncertain whether this method was used prior to this time. Certainly other civilizations had functional calendars as early as the 4th century BCE, so it is easy to assume that the Germanic tribes also had similar technology.

Suggestively, there may have been another means of time keeping: the *golden hats*. The four golden hats are 3,000 years old, dating from 1400-800 BCE. All of them were found in central Europe; specifically, two in present-day Germany, one from central France, and one from Switzerland. One of the golden hats found in Germany still had the leather chin strap in place. Covered with sun and moon symbols these finely wrought and ornate objects date from the Nordic Bronze Age and depict 1,735 days in 57 lunations, which amounts to one quarter of the Metonic cycle – some five hundred years before it was developed by Meton (2). According to German archaeologists and historians these golden cone-shaped hats are part of the ceremonial garb of Bronze Age priestly Time Keepers or oracles. Seemingly, their ability to calculate time, based on logarithmic configurations, and so calculate celestial and terrestrial events, could have been viewed as divine power. Dr. Wilfried Menghin, director of the Berlin Museum, has done extensive research on this subject and compares the golden hats to other time keeping objects and structures around the world (3). Specifically, European models include the Sun Observatory of Goseck, Newgrange in Ireland, Stonehenge in England, and the Nebra Sky Disk of Germany. Regarding the wearers of the golden hats, Dr. Menghin writes, *"They would have been regarded as Lords of Time who had access to a divine knowledge that enabled them to look into the future. The symbols on the hat are a logarithmic table, which enables the movements of the sun and the moon to be calculated in advance,, [snip] They suggest that Bronze Age man would have been able to make long-term, empirical astrological observations, [snip] ..Our findings suggest that the Bronze Age was a far more sophisticated period in Europe than has hitherto been thought".* Relatedly, Dr. Sabine Gerloff of Erlangen University has concluded that the Gold Cape of Mold, discovered in Wales, was part of the full attire of these 'Lords of Time' (4). Even so, such hats are not unique to Germania. Distinctive garments are suggestive of Indo-European culture, but are also found among the Saami Noiade ('shamans') in Finland, and the L'nu Powwaw ('spiritual leader') of northeastern Canada (an indigenous Algonquian tribe). Certainly, northern Europe is no stranger to unusual hats, as witnessed in the Iron Age horned helmets.

Due to the persistent idea of witches and wizards who wear pointed hats, many scholars feel that, perhaps, these gold hats were the original model of such a symbol – perhaps representing an individual who functioned in a Seiðr-shamanic capacity (5). Later examples of these 'wizard hats' were made of felt or leather. In the Medieval text *Life of Saint Columba*, there is a reference to "Pictish magi" who wear tall pointed hats, and in the *History of Ireland*, it is related that the Celtic Druids were Magi from Scythia who wore conical hats (6). This latter can be further supported by a Scythian rock depiction in Behistun, Persia. In all cases, these cone-shaped hats suggest a functionary philosophical influence from the Caucasian Mountain cultures from 1800-800 BCE.

Perhaps in addition to these hats, the 'Lords of Time' may have also worn a gold cape, such as the example unearthed in Mold, Flintshire, North Wales. Found in 1833, this finely tooled gold cape was draped around the remains of a skeleton; perforations along the upper and lower edges indicated that it was attached to a full-length cape, parts of which were discovered. The design, which was laboriously beaten from a single gold ingot, gives the impression of multiple strings of beads amid folds of cloth. Other objects in the grave included bronze and amber beads (7). Finally, other items of interest that many archeologist believe were emblems of a (mostly) female priestly caste include:
-*belt boxes*, or wide leather belts embossed with bronze or gold disks, 11" in diameter and 3-4" deep;
-*arm rings* with 'eyes', thought to hang items;

-*hooks* for hanging objects from the belt;
-*torc*, decorated with spirals and attached ornamental plates;
-*bronze axes* and *sickles*; and a
-*bronze bra*.
Designs on some of these items depict 6-12 "moons", one or two ships (thought to symbolize the year/half year; 16 such finds total), and all of these objects were found in either Ribe, South Jutland, or Lejfr, Zealand.

## Part Six:  Bronze Age Religion, 1700-500 BCE
Little is known regarding Bronze Age religion, but it can be said with certainty that sun objectification was an integral aspect.  The Bronze Age tribes of Trundholm, Denmark had a beautiful wood wagon, pulled by miniature horses that carried a sundisk.  Other finds during this time include sun ships that resemble the one depicted on the Nebra Disk (in Germany).  Most scholars agree that the sky god Tyr was the most prominent deity during this time, having been recently adopted from the Indo-European pantheon (*tiwaz* is Luwian for 'sun, day').  Many Bronze Age rock carvings depict a 'god' figure with a spear (Tyr?), and another with an axe or hammer (Donar-Thor?; 1).  Likewise, the carved ship patterns upon stones include sunwheels – a circle with an equal-armed cross – which may have been likewise associated with wagon wheels.

Like later periods, outdoor worship – from stone alters to processional ways – play an important role in Bronze Age religion; most votive offerings have been found deposited in small lakes or bogs, inside rock clefts, or atop mountains and hills.  In some bogs there have been found wooden idols that may have served as markers, signifying which deity was the particular guardian of that location.  Weapons, often broke or bent to perhaps deter theft, are found in bogs, as are pottery vessels containing food stuffs, horse riding gear, agricultural tools, and the like (2).  The most common of all Bronze Age offerings, aside from weapons, is lyres, and most of these are found in pairs, and so thought to play a key role in religious rituals.  The golden hats, mentioned above, were all found in bogs, as were gold torcs, which are generally agreed to have been also worn during religious rituals.  Ritual platforms have also been unearthed – wooden tables with four posts, and horn-like tips attached at the corners, pointing upwards.  They may have served as altars and so held weapons, or bound humans who would be sacrificed. Either way, such 'horned' alters were also found in Kivik, southernmost Sweden, from 1400 BCE, and are similar to those found in northern Tyrolia and Greece.

Mounds from the Bronze Age offer the most detailed and complete picture of everyday life, compared to the periods before that. For the first time, folk were being buried in oak coffins and adorned in elaborate costumes, ornate string skirts, and beautifully carved or crafted jewelry. Men were buried with weapons and women's hair was neatly braided and piled high in fancy styles, both are found wearing bronze and gold adornment. These huge mounds and the nearby remains of monumental long houses indicate a farming class community. Fields were plowed for either cultivation or grazing, and many of their work tools have been found; such as the plough and harness. The average farmstead was 300-1000 square meters, and dwellings were either large single houses, or smaller dwellings in groups; both types of sites being inhabited for several centuries.

Cremation graves first appear in the Iron Age, 500 BCE – 700 CE, as do small farmsteads surrounded by fences, and the first indication of organized villages (the signs of an increasingly stratified society). This is also when the first bog bodies appear, such as the Tollund and Grauballe Men. More than likely they were killed and thrown into a bog or water as an offering to the gods. The oldest war booty/offering comes from this time, the Hjortspring find, which is a Danish wood boat – similar to that found depicted on Bronze Age rock carvings – filled with Celtic-made weapons. Likewise, the Dejbjerg Wagons, and the Brå and Gundestrup Cauldrons – also of Celtic origin – come from this period. It was during the Roman Iron Age, 500 BCE-1 CE, that the Germanic Cimbrians and Teutons were roaming northern Europe, attacking the northern boundary of the Roman Empire.

The Golden Horns of Gallehus, from South Jutland in Denmark, with detailed runic inscriptions and artistic design (which were stolen in 1802 CE), dated from the Germanic Iron Age (400-550 CE), a period that was rich in gold coins, neck and arm rings, gold bracteates and plaquettes (depicting men, women, animals, and runes). Most of these finds are concentrated around a central area that no doubt held a central function – such as Sorte Muld in Bornholm, Denmark.

## Part Seven:  Lejra – Home of Nerthus (?)

Northern Europe is known for its chariot or wagon cults, such as Nerthus, Ing-Fro, Freyr, and perhaps Gefion's plough; then there are the wagon and sun-chariot finds of Lejre and Sealand.  By extension, perhaps, we could include the ship on wheels, which is part of the modern-day Aarhus, Jutland annual celebrations of spring.

The continental Danes, their neighbors across the sea, and the Swedes, certainly celebrate a spring, fertility goddess – as is well known from both historical finds and *Ynglinga saga*.  This ritual, known as the Disablot, later became a rite dedicated to a nameless female divine power.  According to *Ynglinga saga*, it was Freya who held the role of *Dis-gydje* and *Hov-gode*, or 'ancestral priestess' and 'temple priestess', during the annual sacrifices in the temple at Sigtuna, Sweden.  Which is something even Tacitus noted when he wrote, "*Of gods they venerated Mercury (Odin) in particular, sacrificing to him humans on special days. To Hercules (Thor) and Mars (Tyr) they sacrificed animals. Some of the Svebians (Swedes) also sacrificed to Isis (Nerthus or Freya); the origins of this cult I have been unable to find, except that the image of the goddess is found in the likeness of a ship, indicating that this religion may have come to them by the sea.*"  (Parenthesis, my own)

Again, from the Lore, we know that there were five full moon celebrations: Winter Night in October; Yule in December; Disthing in March; Summer Night in June; and, Harvest in August.  Of them all, Disthing was considered the single-most important of all because everyone – both low and highborn, participated (the seven tribes that Tacitus mentions could have easily come together for this one celebration).   The reason for this is that the Disthing was a "parliament of the people", and based on Tactitus' account of this one event, in which all seven tribes would converge, many have speculated that its location was at Lejre, a town and municipality in modern-day Zealand (or Sjælland); today, an island belonging to Denmark.  In Old Norse, the town was known as Hleiðra, and there is some speculation that it was the location of Heirot Hall, from the epic tale *Beowulf*.  Whatever the case may be, Lejre is also the location of a great many neck and arm rings, gold plates, twelve engraved moon circles, two metal-cast ships, several wood ships, innumerable weapons, jewelry, and other votive offerings.

Most scholars agree that Lejre is the most likely location of the "island" where Nerthus' worship was carried out. This location is not chosen merely on the number of artifacts found but also due to it being the location where the Kings of Wessex trace their ancestry; specifically from *Scyld*, or *Skjöldr*, who was the first of the legendary Danish Kings. Both the lineages and history are mentioned in the *Prose Edda, Ynglinga saga, Chronicon Lethrense*, the history of Sven Aggesen, *Skjöldunga saga*, and Saxo's *Gesta Danorum*. All of these accounts agree that Scyld is one of Wodan's sons; and they also relate that Wodan came from the Black Sea, conquered Northern Europe, and gave Sweden to his son Yngvi, and Denmark to his son Skjöldr. Ever since then, the Kings of Sweden have been known as the Ynglings and the Kings of Denmark as the Skjöldungs (Scyldings).

In *Beowulf*, Scyld Scefing is a Danish king – progenitor of the Danish royal line – and descendant of *Scef*, or *Scyld of the Sheaf*; who, according to legend, was cast adrift as a small child in a boat. Some scholars have seen similarities with Scyld's story to that of *John Barleycorn* of later Anglo-Saxon folksongs, and the Finnish *Pekko*, a god of crops and brewing, and eventually *Bergelmir*, from the *Eddas* (1). It may be recalled that Bergelmir was considered a Jotun who survived the flood of *Aurgelmir's* blood, in a ship with his wife, to become the progenitor of a new race of giants. Finally, after King Frode Fredegod died, his companions embalmed his body, placed it in a wagon, and sent it through the countryside so his folk could see him. This practice, though considered 'odd' or 'unusual' today, was the manner in which such great leaders were deified. Eventually his body was buried in Lejre, near a famous center of worship. As such, many scholars believe the myths regarding Gefn, Baldr, King Skjold, and King Frode can all be considered linked to the Nerthus cult.

## Part Eight: Germanic and Slavic Goddesses of Light and Darkness

*"The most important description of the peoples whom the Romans called Germans is in Tacitus's work.."* Both *Germania* and the *Annals* are considered reliable resources in that many of the events chronicled there have been validated through archeological proofs. If Tacitus' account can be said to be valid in the above statement (and several others), can it not also be said to be valid in regards to Nerthus as a *goddess* who received human sacrifice?

Today, in Poland, the *Drowning of Marzanna* is celebrated to 'bury the winter' and 'welcome the spring' (1). Marzanna is mentioned in a medieval Christian text known as the *Mater Verborum*, or Mother Inspiration, where she is compared to *Hecate*, the Anatolian Mother Goddess of Death, the wilderness, liminal spaces, sorcery, and lovingly referred to as Queen of Ghosts. Likewise, Marzanna's name is from the Slavic root *mor* meaning 'nightmare' and 'death'. She is thought to symbolize the sun, so that an effigy of her is either burnt or drowned on the last day of the festivities, which often last for seven days. Bulgarian Mythology depicts her as *Baba Marta* ('grandma'), a grumpy old woman. In her seasonal celebration they gift each other with small wool dolls adorned with red and white ribbon (semen and blood) – pinned to clothing, worn in the hair, or attached to fruit-bearing trees, 'to please Baba Marta so that she will not make winter last'. The animal associated with her is the *stork*, a traditional harbinger of spring (and 'bringer' of babies). Divination is an integral aspect of her worship today; for example, red ribbons symbolize the setting sun of spring, which becomes more intense as the Vernal Equinox approaches, and white ribbons symbolize purity and melting snow. In all, these rites represent health and joy, conception and new life, fertility and abundance.

In Russia this celebration is known as *Maslenitsa* or Pancake Week (February 16-22) – a sun festival that celebrates the end of winter. Traditional foods include the *bliny* or Russian pancakes made with butter, eggs and milk, and eaten with caviar, fresh cream, honey and lots of butter. In fact, the word 'Maslenitsa' is derived from Russian *maslo*, meaning 'butter'. Other activities include war games between men, egg decorating for children, puppet plays that relate folklore, and lots of eating. A common saying is, *"Have as many meals as a dog wags its tail!*" A straw effigy is made of Lady Maslenitsa – the Maslenitsa Doll – who, at the end of the festivities, is stripped of her finery and either thrown into a fire or drowned. If burnt, her ashes are sprinkled on barren earth "for a heavy crop". This last day is considered an opportunity to mend relationships by reconciling old grudges.

In Latvia she is the Goddess *Mara*, patroness of crops and children, of wealth and health, who takes our body upon death, caring for them in death. Mara is an ancient goddess of the land, a *Māras zeme* or tribal goddess. The Polabian Slavs, who lived along the Elbe, in modern-day Germany, between the Baltic Sea and modern-day Poland, honored *Šiwa / Šiva* (*sheva; Zisa?*) – tribal goddess of "living, being, existing" (2). In fact, it is tempting here to consider Zisa, Tyr's companion and consort, as the "Isis" of the Suebi, that Tacitus mentions; Grimm certainly made that connection. Either way, the *Chronica Slavorum* I:52, lists her as the "supreme goddess", her main cult center being in Ratzeburg – located in Schleswig-Holstein, in northern Germany (3). A town situated in the middle of four lakes, which leave narrow access paths to the town. In a medieval Czech dictionary her name is said to be synonymous with earth, specifically, "alive and vital", and she is said to "open her body (the earth) to everything and everybody".

Among the Lithuanians and Latvians she is *Saule,* whose name means, "sun". She is the Queen of Heaven and Earth whose celebration is at the end of the winter solstice and again at the summer solstice. As a Sun Goddess, she is also recognized at the equinoxes. In many ways she appears similar to how many Germanic Heathens envision *Sunna*. Saule is said to have golden hair, gold silk clothing, a gold crown, and she drives a golden chariot across the sky, pulled by two horses called *Asviniai*, Gods of the Shining Sky. She is also threaded to the sea, for it is said that she sinks below the waves every evening to bathe herself and wash her steeds. At night she is said to visit the Underworld, where her dark aspect becomes Queen of the Dead. According to scholars, it was the Lithuanians who named the planets (long before the Romans), where they recognized Saule as the Mother of Planets. Her daughters are:
*Vaivora* / Mercury;

*Ausrine* / Venus, the Morning Star;
*Zemyna* / Earth;
*Ziezdre* / Mars;
*Selija* / Saturn; and,
*Indraja* / Jupiter. Saula is said to 'dance with her daughters at the winter and summer solstices. Once married to *Menulis*, the Moon, she left him because he took their daughter Ausrine, the Dawn, as wife. For this reason Saule scarred Menulis' face – which is why the moon is pocked and marked. Because she is single, she is beloved to single women and widows.

Saula is said to keep a garden of golden apples, a bright perpetual flame, her horses, snakes, roses and daisies, a white cow, and a white and black she-goat – these latter represent her day and night aspect. She also keeps bees, burning solar wheels, and tends the World Tree, which is named after her: *Saule's Medis* (Saule's Tree). Her burning sun wheels are known as *ridolele* or 'rolling sun', or simply *rota*, 'to roll'. On the morning of summer solstice, Lithuanians rise before the sun so as not to 'miss Saule's first healing and blessed rays'. Latvian songs relate, *"The sun, dancing on the silver hill, has silver shoes on her feet."* For many she is the only god, the true guardian of her folk, and all aspects of woman's work falls under her watch – such as blessing of the fields, healing, and playing the *kankle* (a traditional stringed instrument; 4).

## Part Nine: Creating a Modern Heathen Nerthus Rite
A great deal of information has been presented regarding Nerthus, the circumstances of her worship, the possible examples of her existence in Paganism across Old Europe, and even today. What remains is combining these elements together into a workable format for modern Heathens.

In that human sacrifice is not an option, the significance of sacrifice must suffice. As has been shown, such acts were meant to benefit tribe, sending a 'whole' body to the goddess for her to use in a manner befitting her function. In return, the tribe received a blessing through the promise of fertility and abundance. Seemingly then, a moderated and observable outline of *self-sacrifice*, over the course of a year (from Disthing to Disthing) could be an opportunity for an individual, a family, kindred or tribe to honor Nerthus, receive her rich blessings, and afford one of its folk an opportunity to 'sacrifice' their life for the good of tribe. This can be accomplished via proscribed deeds that **must** be carried out by the willing 'sacrifice', then witnessed and agreed upon by family / kindred / tribal chieftains / leaders in good standing. Twelve proposed deeds of *self-sacrifice* are:

| Male Deeds | Female Deeds |
| --- | --- |
| Oath yourself to Nerthus for one year, 'sacrificing' yourself to the completion of the deeds below to honor Nerthus and bring blessing to kindred / tribe. | Oath yourself to Nerthus for one year, 'sacrificing' yourself to the completion of the deeds below to honor Nerthus and bring blessing to kindred / tribe. |
| | |
| Chop a cord of wood and have it ready for use at a large public moot. | Bake several loaves of homemade bread and handmade butter to be served at a large public moot. |
| | |
| Become skilled in a weapon and teach a class on this weapon at a large public moot. | Weave or knit a shawl or comforter to be gifted or sold at auction at a large public moot. |
| | |
| Make a significant home improvement to your own home or the home of a kindred member. (Example: install gutters or a roof vent, replace a window, landscaping, bleach or paint a building's exterior, etc.) | Sew a traditional Heathen woman's dress to be gifted or sold at auction during a large public moot. |
| | |
| Read an Edda or Saga that you are not familiar with and present a class on it, with handouts, at a large public moot. | Read an Edda or Saga that you are not familiar with and present a class on it, with handouts, at a large public moot. |
| | |
| Make a batch of mead that will be used at the *next* Nerthus' Faining. | Make a batch of mead that will be used at the *next* Nerthus' Faining. |
| | |

| | |
|---|---|
| Provide a hoofed meal for one large public moot (examples: roast pig, steaks, venison, etc – either hunted or purchased). | Cultivate a vegetable and/or herb garden and donate the produce for one large public moot. |
| Create fire by traditional/primitive means, without the use of matches, gas, or lighter, etc. | Make an herbal soap, candle, shampoo, salve, etc, and present it as a gift or auction at a large public moot. |
| Be original! Devise your own task that can be presented as a class, a gift, or auction item at a large public moot. | Be original! Devise your own task that can be presented as a class, a gift, or auction item at a large public moot. |
| Compose a poem or song to Nerthus, and publicly recite it at a large public moot. | Compose a poem or song to Nerthus, and publicly recite it at a large public moot. |
| Build a Hörgr to the ancestors and dedicate it over the course of three nights by spending a minimum of three hours a night – for three consecutive nights – in front of it. | Build a Hörgr to the ancestors and dedicate it over the course of three nights by spending a minimum of three hours a night – for three consecutive nights – in front of it. |
| Create a personal Nerthus symbol that will be donated to and so become a permanent accompaniment to a Nerthus Wagon. | Create a personal Nerthus symbol that will be donated to and so become a permanent accompaniment to a Nerthus Wagon. |

-Each deed is an **oathed** deed that must be accomplished over the course of a year, so that all deeds are completed on a timely basis, to conclude a year from when the blot began (Disthing).
-Each deed must be witnessed and approved by a chieftain / leader of a Heathen family or kindred in good standing, to be deemed suitable for both Nerthus and the benefit of tribe.

-If the *self-sacrifice* is unable to attend a large public moot, they must prove their worth by presenting their oath to a local family or kindred chieftain / leader.

In closing, recall that this format has been successfully carried out, so based on one's individual sincerity, the self-sacrifice should be accepted.  However, my personal success – based on almost four decades of Seiðwork, and that of a Seið-colleague (three decades) – may not be indicative of other results.

~ ~ ~

## References

**Nerthus: A Germanic Goddess of Death and Tribal Blessing**
Written in 2007 for an Asatru / Heathen Moot in Florida; revised in 2010, and 2017.  Presented at 'Lunch and Lore' (a monthly meeting of area Heathens in central Georgia); at Southlands Moot (a regional Georgia moot); and at Osprey Bay Kindred (2007; Florida). Presented at the 'Temple of Isis' in Alabama, at 'Bell, Book, and Candle' in North Carolina, and Augusta Pagan Pride in Georgia (2010-2011).

**Part One: Terra Mater**
1-1 Samuel 6:7-10; 2 Samuel 6:6, 7; 1 Chronicles 13:9, 10.

2-Simek, R., *Dictionary of Northern Mythology*, 1984.

3-All Indo-European references are from *The American Heritage Dictionary Indo-European Roots Index*, 2000.

4-Lincoln, B., *Death, War, and Sacrifice*, 1991.
Güntert, H., *Kalypso, Bedeutungsgeschichtliche Untersuchungen auf dem Gebiet der indogermanischen Sprachen*, 1919.

5-Men's names: Ingimundr, Ingifast, Ingjaldr, Ingivaldr, Ingólfr, Yngvar.  Women's names: Inga, Ingeborg, Ingriðr, Ingiþóra, Ynghildr, Yngona.

6-Deil, P., *Le Symbolisme dans la mythologie grecque*; page 120-129; 1952.

7-Burket, W., *Greek Religion*; section 3.3, 4; 1982.

8-Mallory, J.P., *In Search of the Indo-Europeans: Language, Archaeology and Myth*, page 27; 1989.

9-Motz, L., *The Goddess Nerthus: A New Approach,* from Amsterdamer Beitrage zur Alteren Germanistik, Bd 36; 1992.

**Part Three:  Eleven Observations**
1-Simek, R. (see ref; 2 above), and Rybakov, B., *The Scythia of Herodotus: historico-geographical analysis*, 1979, pages 23-34, 112-113.

2-Lund University (Sweden), underwater Stone Age site.  *A submerged Mesolithic lagoonal landscape in the Baltic Sea, south-eastern Sweden – Early Holocene environmental reconstruction and shore-level displacement based on a multiproxy approach*, 2016, Paper presented at the Quaternary International annual meeting.

**Part Four:  Human Sacrifice**
1-Mallory, J.P., *In Search of the Indo-Europeans: Language, Archaeology and Myth*, page 199; 1989.

2-Yogatrayananda, *Siva-ratri*, page 171; 1936.

3 and 3a-Bord, J. and C., *Sacred Waters*, page 124; 1985.

4-Hutton, R., BBC article:
http://www.digitaljournal.com/article/33600/Harry_Potter_Fever_Prompts_Britons_To_Probe_Magical_Past)

5-Glob, P., *The Bog People: Iron-Age Man Preserved*, 2004

**Part Five:  Keeping Time**
1-Steele, J. M., *Observations and Predictions of Eclipse Times by Early Astronomers*, 2000.

2-Toomer, G. J., *Dictionary of Scientific Biography*, section: Meton.

3-Menghin, W., *Magisches Gold. Kultgerät der späten Bronzezeit*, 1977

4-Gerloff, S., *Bronzezeitliche Goldblechkronen aus Westeuropa: Betrachtungen zur Funktion der Goldblechkegel vomTyp Schifferstadt und der atlantischen, Goldschalen' der Form Devil's Bit und Atroxi*, pages 161-188, 1995

5-Reference *Part Two: Terra Mater*, Cybele's high cylindrical hat.

6-Fletcher, R., *Who's Who in Roman Britain and Anglo-Saxon England*, 1989.
And, Moore, T., *The History of Ireland: Commencing with Its Earliest Period, to the Great Expedition Against Scotland in 1545*, Volume 1, section: *Picts*, 1843

7-Powell, T. G. E., *The Gold Ornament from Mold, Flintshire, North Wales*, lecture, Prehistoric Society 19, 1953. Also, National Museum Cardiff:
https://museum.wales/cardiff/whatson/6735/The-Mold-Gold-Cape/

## Part Six: Bronze Age Religion, 1700-500 BCE

1-Litsleby Rock Carving, Vitlycke Museum and Tanum World Heritage Center, Tanushede, Sweden.
Goldhahn, J., *Engraved Biographies: Rock Art and Life-Histories*, academic paper, 2014.
Kristiansen, K. 1987. *Centre and Periphery in Bronze Age Scandinavia*, 1987, pages 74-85.

2-Wells, P.S., *The Battle that Stopped Rome*, pages 32, 42.
Another explanation of why weapons were broken or bent is given by Roy Baehr, a modern-day Seiðman. Specifically: ".. *due to the fact that one could not own a sword unless they were a Kon (King) or Jarl (Earl), or a champion gifted one by a Kon or Jarl (this would become the later medieval knight class). Having a sword meant you were a man of renown. So to prevent a descendant from claiming renown he had not earned, the sword was rendered unusable – the*

*young man would have to build renown of his own and claim his own sword. This building of renown not only bolstered the family name, but strengthened his personal hammingja both for this, and his next, life."*

**Part Seven: Lejra – Home of Nerthus (?)**
1-25-Mallory, J. P., *In Search of the Indo-Europeans*, page 27
Herbert, K., *Looking for the Lost Gods of England*, 1994.
Tolkien, J.R.R., *Beowulf: A Translation and Commentary*, 2014
Wright, V., *Voluspa: Seidr as Wyrd Consciousness*, pages 21 and 42, 2005

**Part Eight:   Germanic and Slavic Goddesses of Light and Darkness**
1-Marjanić, M., *The Dyadic Goddess and Duotheism in Nodilo's The Ancient Faith of the Serbs and the Croats*, 2003, pdf.
http://sms.zrc-sazu.si/En/SMS6/Marjanic6.html

2-Grimm, J., *Teutonic Mythology*, page 296, 1882.

3-Helmold, *Chronica Sclavorum* (Chronicle of the Slavs), written 1120 CE, published work from 1868.

4-Dainius, S., *The Lithuanian Sun Goddess Saula*, Romuva USA, issue #4; 1991.

# Runic Black Magic: The Germanic Grimoires

*Weladuds sa that briutith*
*An insidious death to he who breaks this.*
-Björketorp Runestone

## The Nature of Magic

The idea of menacing magic is not new; examples exist from ancient times, from the early Jewish magicians, to the Egyptian lector priests, and the Mesopotamian *asipu*. Among the Old European tribes, examples of magic are found within every aspect of life, from *forn threifa* ('ancient healing touch') to memorial rune stones, from small amulets to lorica (personal rune/prayer books), and even etched upon cooking utensils. Likewise, curses are equally prevalent.

Throughout the bewildering richness of textual tradition that is the framework of pre-Christian, Old European history, there is an essential character of the supernatural in every aspect of life. As such, there are numerous examples of the innately intimate perspective of magic among the Heathens of yore, existing as it does in the landscape, equally as it occurs within all living things. When reading the sagas, or the historical accounts of the Scandinavian, Germanic, Celtic, and Slavic tribes, the presence of the mystical and mysterious unfolds on every page. Likewise, the role of women as magic users – as Völvas and Trollwives, as Seeress' and Forn Threifa Healers – whose roles were both deed and character based; meaning, the moral and ethical qualities that formed their individual nature, where both actively acted upon and duly noted by those around them.

By and large, magic, or specifically, Seiðr was the realm of women, in several capacities. Some women did magic solely to benefit themselves or other women, while others did so to benefit their brothers, fathers, lovers or husbands. In many examples, these magic-women assist or hinder the hero by bolstering their strength or endowing them with magical protection, by creating obstacles to prevent them from attaining their goal or provide challenges for him to be further tested (peorth). In every example, these are portraits of women who move beyond the normally applied confines of the academically accepted role of women in society, namely as care providers, mothers, and nurses. Heathen lore is overflowing with tales of strong magical women who decide their own fate, and in so doing were labeled as "witch" and "harlot" by the newly arrived Christian faith.

According to the first Christian missionaries, these women were "transgressors", meaning "violators of law and God's commandments." (*) As such, their magical deeds, whether it be to harm or heal, were generically labeled as "sin", and their noble deeds reduced to not but "black magic". But was their behavior considered ill by their own kin and kith? Were they crossing the boundaries of tribal custom, thew or law? How did the Old European tribes view 'beneficial' and 'bad' magic?

**Morals and Ethics**
Generally speaking, morals are personal and ethics are communal. For example, morals are the accepted codes of conduct that make up an individual's perspective; whereas ethics are the mutually agreed upon principles that govern a culture or group. In that Christianity is based upon Judaic tribal custom and law, it only makes sense that its ideas of 'right' and 'wrong' would be different from those of the Old European or Heathen tribes.

The *Modern / Western worldview* of morals and ethics has been shaped by the 16th century philosopher René Descartes, who wrote extensively on the division of the cosmos into two realities:
-the supernatural world of god, angels, and demons, and
-the natural material world of humans, animals, plants, and matter.
This manner of thinking created two views of magic:

-First, the denial of the supernatural world, and reduction of reality within the natural world as it can be studied by science, and

-Second, the view of magic as existing only in god, angels, and demons (who are engaged in a cosmic battle upon earth and in heaven).

For humans, this means every day events are best approached and explained through science and technology. So that, today, many will pray to god for personal salvation, then turn to modern medicine for healing, then psychology for deliverance from demonic possession or evil influences.

The *Tribal worldview* of the Old Europeans was that divinity and magic were one-in-the-same, or that both were found in a singular breath. Heathens knew the world to be populated with beings such as gods and ancestors, trolls and giants, fairies, ghosts, and animal guides, and that all of these could be used for personal power and gain. Likewise, they knew that these entities would harm those who opposed or neglected them, and bless those who remembered and honored them. In short, the Tribal worldview is an animistic one, where the magic-user (Seið endowed individual) is needed to create alliances with all these beings; **alliances that had very pronounced ethnic and territorial perimeters**. So that magic was not a matter of 'good' and 'bad' but 'us' versus 'them'; or in the language of Heathenry, the *Innangard* and *Utangard* (OE *in-yard* and *out-yard*; -*yard* being "the ground that immediately adjoins or surrounds a house, public building, or recognized outdoor area"). Therefore, one's tribal gods and ancestors, trolls and giants, fairies, ghosts, and animal guides were often in battle with those entities of another tribe. Throughout ancient history, war is the result of one tribe's gods and ancestors defeating the gods and ancestors of another tribe. And because territory is integral to both magic and Seiðr, a defeated tribe was expected to accept the 'new' gods and ancestors of their conquerors, effectively shifting their allegiance to those entities that were apparently more powerful.

Finally, there is the *Indo-European worldview*, which is the precursor of the Tribal worldview (the Indo-Europeans being the pre-Christian, non-Judaic tribes of the Caspian steppes, Anatolia, the Aegean, the Iranian plateau, and Eastern and Western Europe [from the Neolithic era]). In the IE model, the gods battle for control of *All Worlds*, ever seeking to establish the rule of righteousness and order (Xártus; Ṛta). Here, humans stand in the midst of this cosmic struggle, and in the tribal model above, 'good' is associated with 'our side' and the 'other side' is 'bad' because they are against 'us'.

Central to this worldview is the idea of *restorative violence*, or the idea of ransoming / buying back one's rightful might (1). So that magic / Seiðr was a way to redeem one's property, or to buy back one's luck. The example of the exchange of hostages among the Aesirian and Vanirian gods of Heathen lore was the means of establishing balance between two warring tribes, or the creation of a better society (2). As such, morals and ethics among the IE tribes (or the tribes of Old Europe) were not based on the idea of moral rightness, as seen in the Modern/Western/Christian model, but of fairness and opportunity. In regards to Seiðr/magic, to be *fair* meant that it was exchanged between those of **equal** might, allowing for an uncertain outcome or where it would be clear who the gods and ancestors favored. For example, if a powerful Seiðwoman, working alone, used magic against any ordinary farmer, then this would be deemed 'evil' or 'bad'; but if the same Seiðwoman, working with her tribe, used magic against another tribe, and won, then justice and victory had been gained. From the Modern/Western/Christian perspective, all magic is 'evil', seething with violence and deceit; but to the tribes of Old Europe, chaos was 'bad' and might and order were 'good'.

From these examples it can be seen that the Tribal/IE model remains mostly today in the Modern/Western/Christian world through entertainment. For example, books and movies are filled with tales of the cosmic battle being played out between Cowboys and Indians, between rival sports teams, between Superman and Lex Luther, between Luke Skywalker and the Evil Empire, and between Harry Potter and Voldemort.

Today, within the general Pagan magic community, there exists little in-depth research into pre-Christian morals and ethics (or, correctly, Early Pagan Morals and Ethics). As such, strife and turmoil are viewed as a matter of 'good' versus 'bad'; which results in individuals and/or groups, when confronted with adversity, 'casting a circle', invoking the 'white light' and sprinkling salt, all to gain protection, personal salvation or deliverance from 'dark/bad/evil' influences. This manner of thinking belongs to the Christian perspective, or the perceived conquerors of the Old European tribes; meaning, many Pagans today have conceded defeat through default of the Modern/Western worldview. On the otherhand, the Heathen magic user – Seiðr or Runic – must acquire skill through constant application of will; and if one's efforts are diligent, they may gain might, recognition and support through the gods, Nattura, and personal ancestors, who all bolster familial luck. Based on dedication and diligence then, and only then, is one in a position to represent their tribe, to seek out powerful alliances, and to establish and maintain perimeters to assure that the Innangard is made whole and holy, while the Uttangard is kept at bay – by strong Seiðr/magic if necessary.

## The Nature of Cursing

The word *curse* is English and dates to the 9th century; it is rooted in Proto-Germanic *bannan*, meaning, "proclaim, command, forbid" (it is further seen in *banish*, *expel*). Older still it has a Proto-Indo-European root, *bha*, meaning "to speak", which relates to Old Irish *bann* / "law". As such, the word ties-in with the Tribal Worldview of 'commanding' the gods and ancestors to do what is *right*, and to 'forbid' that which is out/Utangard from coming in/Innangard. Further, it clearly relates that this is something spoken and even 'lawful', denoting the might and order of the Old European Weltanschauung of right / righteousness. Finally, and again from linguistics, a curse was meant to have a *causative* result.

Undoubtedly, the early Church sought to eradicate the competition from foreign gods, and because magic was innate to the Heathen tribes – being the primary means of communication within their respective environment/territory – it was deemed 'bad' or 'black magic'. Today, the term *black magic* generally conjures up images of malevolent practices and nefarious deeds, of misfortune and death, of sickness and injury. In short, it has become synonymous with 'evil'; a situation which then gave birth to 'white magic' or all that is allegedly good and beneficial.

Cursing is found throughout Heathen Literature, from the Irish-Welsh tale of *Tristan and Iseult* – where the queen curses Morholt's slayer, and the island of England (an example of protecting the Innangard against the Utangard); to the English-Welsh *Percival saga* – where the Loathly Lady curses Percival's quest (an example of the magic woman and the hero). In that this is an essay specifically on the Runes, we will look to the numerous examples of Runic Cursing.

## Germanic Grimoires, or The Art of Cursing
Heathenry has several books of Rune magic, dating from the 14th to the 19th centuries, a period of time denoting both the continuity and popularity of these powerful texts. Combined, they contain a wide array of folk knowledge, from herbal lore to healing stones (to include those used in forn threifa (1), from magical songs to amulets, from calendars with auspicious dates to the making of poppets, from the evil eye to protection prayers, from mystic chants to invoke gods to love spells, from magic wands to cursing tablets, and from divination methods to other mystic arts. The most notable of these Grimoires are:

-*Handritið Huld*, the 'Secret Handwriting', written in 1847 by Geir Vigfússyni, contains over 300 examples of Runic magic, written in both known and secret/coded Runic scripts. The text contains over 30 bindrunes, most of which dealing with establishing and maintaining sacred space, dream magic, creating both good and ill luck, means to create terror and fear, to open locked doors, several Rune Galdrs to kill someone, Runes for scrying, for winning a law suit, for invisibility, and how to sway a court of law in your favor.

*-Hlíðarendabók*, the 'Hills Edge Book', written during the early 1500s by Visa Gisli. Notably, this text is bound in red leather and also contains *Jónsbók*, or 'John the Lawspeaker's Book', a collection of law codes from the 11<sup>th</sup> century. Here, virtually every page contains a Runic incantation to aid in carrying out the law; indicating once again the Tribal practice of magic/Seiðr being used to protect right and cosmic order.

*-Galdrakverfrá*, the 'Incantation Songs', written during the middle 1500s by an unknown author. This text contains the galdrastafir of the gods, several love charms, healing formulas (forn threifa), how to create fear and dread in an enemy, the calendar days of bad luck, how to make people vomit and fart, how to kill an enemy's livestock, how to find a thief, how to win a legal case, how to make someone fall into a permanent sleep, how to raise the dead, how to gather fish into your net, how to make an man impotent, and many other useful charms.

*-Manuscript 143*, from the University of Iceland Theological Library, written during the early part of the 17<sup>th</sup> century by an unknown author. This text contains Runic amulets and charms with Christian elements. The Conversion did not mean the overnight destruction of the ancient Heathen traditions, but the retention of many local customs and cultural expressions. In this case, containing examples of early Christian mysticism, such as the supernatural names of god, the letters and numbers of the Cabalistic system, the use of phylacteries (amulets worn on the body containing Heathen and Christian expressions), lorica, prayers and exorcisms, healing charms (forn threifa galdr), the *Greenland Fish Amulet* (used as a prayer counter, written in Runes), and other Gnostic devices. Notably, this Grimoire contains two charms written in Runes, meant to bring about Christian dominance:
*-Stafirnir fjórir*, the 'Four Staves' that promise to "stand the galdr of all four sides, to bear down the cross".
*-Róðukrossinn*, the 'Pole Cross' that promises to "use a shaft against our enemies that they don't suspect us."
Undeniably, these are examples of Christian magic using the Tribal perspective of magic/ Seiðr to seek right and order against a territorial enemy.

-*Manuscript 247*, from the Árni Magnússon Institute, written during the early 1800s CE by an unknown author. This collection of pages contains spells to protect one's self from thieves, to make vendors give you a good deal, and inscriptions to keep a knife from breaking. Notably, this Grimoire contains the *Munnlaugarstafur* or the 'Murmuring Water Staves', to assist in dreamwork and scrying; and the S*já Stjörnur um Daga*, or how to 'See Stars by Day' charm.

-*Rauðskinni*, the *Red Skin*, written circa 1640 by Gottskálk Niklásson, Bishop of Hólar, a well-established Christian magician. Gottskálk the Cruel, also, Gottskálk the Sinister, was said to have compiled the vilest of all magics – drawn from both Heathenry and Christianity – and wrote them in gold runes upon bloodied parchment. To assure that no one would ever know his secrets, he ordered the book buried with him. The text was said to contain instructions on *Galdramyndir* or shape-shifting, how to conjure giants and trolls to do one's bidding, to control the forces of nature, and necromancy.

According to legend, after Gottskálk's death, a magician named Loptur, at the school in Hólar, decided to retrieve the infamous *Book of the Red Skin*. Breaking into the burial mound he used his skill to raise the specter of Gottskálk, which commenced to curse him; and though Loptur managed to escape with the book, he was made mad by the experience. Today, there exists no known knowledge of the books physical existence.

-*Gráskinni*, the *Gray Skin*, written in the late 1600s, by Halfdánur Narfason, the Vicar of Fell, who was the 'good' to Gottskálk's 'bad' (see *Red Skin* above). During this period there were two towns with magical universities: Hólar and Skalholt. According to historical texts at both locations, the *Gray Skin* was said to be written in both Latin and *Villurúnir*, or 'Wild Runes', and contain incantations for developing physical strength, mental acuity, healing (forn theifa), divination (spá / spæ / spae) and palmistry (lófalist). According to legend, anyone reading the Latin section of the book would enter heaven, and those who read the *Wild Runes*, would be damned. Loptur the Galdrmann was said to have read the second half of the Gray Skin, and it was this section, written in the Villurúnir, that aided him in raising the ghost of Gottskálk.

### The Art of Cursing, Part Two

There are numerous examples of cursing in Germanic lore:

-*Áliflekks saga*, the 'Saga of Áli the Marked', where Áli and his family are bothered by a band of trolls, prompting Áli to exchange numerous curses with them. Some examples include turning a troll into a stone slab, turning a human into a wolf, a curse to make one scream uncontrollably, a curse to cause wounds to appear without being physically attacked, and curses to cause constant nightmares. Notably, the curse found here – or Runic incantation – is to transform a human into a wolf (1).

-*Bósa saga ok Herrauds*, the 'Saga of Bósi and Herraud', where is found the most powerful of all Runic curses. *Busla's Curse* is such that it was feared that, even read after the fact, it retained the power to cause injury. Busla was a powerful Seiðwoman who cursed the king of Östergötland when he refused to release her foster son Bósa, who had been wrongfully accused of murder. It remains today as a template for all other curses.

-*Göngu-Hrólfs saga*, the 'Saga of Strolling Hrólf', where Princess Ingigerd is cursed to live as a troll until a human man falls in love and lays with her.

-*Gríms saga loðinkinna*, the 'Saga of Grim Shaggy-Cheek', where Grimhild turns her stepdaughter into a troll.

-*Grottasöngr*, the 'Song of Grótti', relates how the Gýgjar, Fenja and Menja, curse King Frodi for his arrogance of their noble birth (2).

-*Hálfdanar saga Eysteinssonar*, the 'Saga of Hálfdanar Eysteinssonar', where Grim curses Halfdan into marrying her, even though he had never met her. The curse then was that Halfdan was driven mad with longing until he found her.

-*Helgakviða Hjörvarðssonar*, the 'Lay of Helgi Hjörvarðsson', a troll woman curses Helgi for not laying with her. Then, as a continuation of this saga: *Helgakviða Hundingsbana*, the 'Lay of Helgi Hundingsbane', where Svava curses her brother for killing her lover, Helgi.

-*Hervarar saga ok Heiðreks*, the 'Saga of Valkyrie Hervar, and Heidreck', where the Valkyrie Hervar curses her father, Angantyr, who at the time was dead. The powerful Seiðwoman Hervar journeyed to the Realm of the Dead, gained entrance, called forth her father from his Mound, and demanded he yield his sword to her. He refused, so she cursed him to torment. Fearful of a continued existence in Hel suffering with anguish and pain, he relinquished the sword, and Hervar was able to claim her inheritance. Notably, this saga was the inspiration for J.R.R. Tolkien in his creation of the *Lord of the Ring* epic.

-*Hrólfr Kraki saga*, the 'Saga of King Hrólf Kraki', where a beautiful princess is cursed with ugliness, and where the Seiðwoman Skuld curses Bjorn to become a bear. In this instance, the curse became a family trait, so that all of Bjorn's children had the ability to transform into bears, and while in human form, had great strength (3).

-*Illuga saga Gríðarfóstra*, the 'Saga of Illugi, Grida's Foster son', where Illugi encounters a troll who was once an Elf woman, cursed by a Seidwoman who was jealous of her beauty.

-*Þorsteins saga Víkingssonar*, the 'Saga of Thorstein, a Viking's Son', where Jokul curses the kings' daughter, Ingeborg, causing her to become a hideous troll.

-*Völsungasaga*, the 'Saga of the Völsungs', has several examples of cursing: of Gudrun cursing Gjukis for killing Sigurd, and also cursing Atli for breaking his oath to Gunnar; of Byrnhild cursing a group of conniving / "gossiping" women; of Oddrun cursing Atli's mother for killing Gunnar; and of Kraka cursing her fosterparents when she discovers how they deceived her.

In every example above, and many more not listed, there is a common format:

1-The curser is successful because they are casting against an equally skilled individual; and

2-The cursee responds with a curse. Next,

3-The cursed individual is little concerned with the curse, accepting it as their fate/Wyrd;

4-Their immediate concern is exacting vengeance.

To be clear, there is a strong distinction between the words *vengeance* and *revenge*; definitions that cast light, yet again, on the difference between the Modern/Western/Christian basis of moral and ethic, and that of the Tribal worldview. For example, using the archaic meaning for both words:

-*vengeance* is the "infliction of injury, hurt and/or humiliation through a curse, on a person, by one who has been harmed by that person"; and

-*revenge* is "to clear from accusation, to free from suspicion through argument and evidence, against one who opposes another."

To the Heathen, once wronged, it is an obligation to retaliate in kind, as opposed to 'turning the other cheek' or waiting for an appeal or apology. According to Heathen thought, might is right; so that whosoever is most loyal and dedicated to the gods and ancestors – the one who always remembers their ways of worship – is the one rewarded with right and weal. It's not a popularity contest among one's friends and associates, but who lives in accord with the divine Xártus / Ṛta of the Old Ways. (4)

You see, to the ancient Heathens, there was nothing more right than Xártus / Ṛta, or "that which is properly joined; order, rule, truth". This is the natural order which regulates and coordinates the operation of the universe and All That Lives. The gods and ancestors all comply with Xártus / Ṛta, or "that which is right, true, properly joined, moving forward/upward, and fitting". Conceptually, from an Indo-European perspective:

-First there is Xártus / Ṛta; below that is

-*Dharma*, or 'that which upholds or supports Xártus / Ṛta'; and below Dharma is

-*Karma*, or the 'action of an individual in relation to Dharma and Xártus / Ṛta.' (5)

Therefore, those who live in accord with Xártus / Ṛta – in this instance: the Old Ways of pre-Christian, Old Europe – never fear a curse, for their life is truly charmed in their remembrance of their gods and ancestors (if they live this way; 6).

**Examples of Rune Curses**

What came to be considered a 'curse' by the Church, could today be viewed as something quite different. Remember, the 'new' and foreign religion of Christianity was in competition with the Old European Old Ways, so in an effort to eradicate its competition, it used such words as 'sin', 'evil', and 'witchcraft' to create fear in subsequent generations. Seidr, Forn Threifa, Galdr, Cunning, and the like, were innate to the Heathens of yore – being the primary means of communication with the world around them – so the Church used its own version of glamor to convince the 'barbarians' to turn away from their ancestral ways. Even so, many examples of Rune formula and bindrunes remain, to include those the early Church used for its own gain. Some examples of tribal 'magic' banned by the Church, and labeled 'evil' include:

-*Win the Favor of Powerful Men*, to bring success in job interviews, court cases, or to favorably influence the police, etc.

-*Against All Kinds of Suffering and Danger*, to protect one's possessions (vehicle, home, or job).

-*Kaupaloki*, to "un-knot the bargain", meaning, a *Deal Closer*; to make a sale, or success in buying and/or selling.

-*Draumstafur*, "Dream Stave", to promote vivid and/or prophetic dreams, to deepen meditation, and communion with inner self.

-*Lukkustafir*, "Luck Stave", to bring about one's family luck, to increase luck, or repel bad luck.

-*Warding Stave*, for personal/bodily protection, to ward oneself from every direction; an individual shield of warding/protection.

-*Victory in Business, Victory over People, Overcome Adversity and Foes*, to bring success to business meetings, during job interviews, for favorable business contracts, or to be rid of bothersome co-workers.

-*Victory in Law Cases*, to win a law suit, or to persuade a judge or jury.

-*Against Hate and Treacherous Deeds*, to harm another who has wronged you, to return one's foul deeds upon them (virtually 'instant' retribution).

-*Against Wrath*, typically, the Helm of Awe, also to gain victory over others, especially if one is to delight in an enemy's downfall.

-*Hinder Unwelcome Intruders*, to protect one's home from unwanted entry.

-*Evocation of the Three Mothers* (the Triple Goddess), to 'cause to appear' (invoke) the presence of the protective Mothers, also used as a vow / oath to willingly remember them.

-*Invocation of Hail*, to 'create the effect' of damage upon a person or thing, to protect a person or thing by creating damage.

## Conclusion

Where one hand holds a blessing, the other holds a curse – this was innate wisdom to the pre-Christian tribes of Old Europe. So the idea of any deed being 'sinister' or 'black magic', would not have been understood among our ancestors if such was used to defend and protect one's hearth and kinsmen. For those who honored the gods and ancestors of their tribe, both harm and heal were but tests or trials (peorth) of their might and dedication. Evenso, the Runes were not meant for every man. In *Havamal*, one of Heathenry's most sacred texts, there is a section solely dedicated to the Runes; therein, those who consider using them are asked:

*Know you how to carve, know you how to interpret?*
*Know you how to paint (grasp), know you how to test (peorth)?*
*Know you how to bid (ask), know you how to sacrifice?*
*Know you how to send, know you how to destroy?*

And in *Egils saga* – Egil being a renowned Rune magician and werewolf – there are many examples of misery and death being the reward of those who use the runes incorrectly. For example, Egil himself warns us:

*No man should carve runes unless he can read them well.*
*Many a man goes astray around those dark letters.*
*On the whalebone I saw ten secret letters carved,*
*from them, the linden tree took her long harm.*
['linden tree' is a kenning or poetic expression for:
hanging tree, spear point, death]

There is nothing from the Heathen world as complex as the Runes; their power being so effective that it was readily employed by Greeks, Romans, and Christians alike. Unlike other forms of 'binding' or 'fixing' magic – where one must physically pierce an object or create a representation of someone through a poppet – Runes need no such actions to make them work (*). Nor is it necessary to call upon gods of the underworld or malevolent spirits to do one's bidding. Runes are powerful in their own right, able to stop a thief, to staunch the flow of blood, or bring forth the dead from their graves. So it is well to remember that the might of Runes is not found by simply drawing them, but by those who seek them in the wild places – among moss and grass, wind and feather. Then, once found, learn to sing them, or, as the lore teaches us: to *widen out from one end* the wise wisdom within.

~ ~ ~

# Reference

**Runic Black Magic: The Germanic Grimoires**
Written in 2012 for 'Unhewn Stone', and 'Unser Weg', both are exclusive Seidr organizations (the former in the United States, the latter in Germany). Likewise, *Unser Weg: Sacred Female Traditions Revealed*, is a book I wrote in 2008, and submitted to the *American Academy of Religion* as a Research Paper. Presented at Savannah Pagan Pride, Atlanta Pagan Pride, OHM Coven (Tennessee, USA), and the German language version presented to Unser Weg in Clausthal-Zellerfeld, Germany.

**Title**
Björketorp Runestone. Seventh century inscription, upon one of the tallest known runestones; Blekinge, Sweden.

**The Nature of Magic**
*Summers, M., *Malleus Maleficarum*, 1486 CE.
Fairfax, E., Daemonologia: A Discourse on Witchcraft, 1621 CE.

**Morals and Ethics**
1-Restorative violence, also restorative justice. The idea that wrongdoing is an offense against an individual or community rather than of the State. The Brehan Law Codes of Ireland, the law codes of King Clovis I of Gaul, and the Laws of Aethelberht of England, all contain examples.
2-Ransom. Hoenir and Mimir were ransomed; likewise, Otr's Ransom.

**Germanic Grimoires**
1-*Forn Threifa: Ancient Healing Touch*, V. Wright, 2016.

**The Art of Cursing, Part Two**
1-*Werewolf: A Northern History and Tradition*, 2007; V. Wright.

2-Gýgjar, meaning, "giantess", but are also listed as goddesses. Gygjar are Keepers of magical objects.

3-Yet another example of skin-skipting, or 'shapeshifting' found in Heathen lore.

4-Vengence and revenge, *Voluspa: Seidr as Wyrd Consciousness*, verse 54; 2005, V. Wright.

5-Karma. As understood in the Modern/Western/Christian-based mentality, karma is, essentially 'what one sows, they reap', or if following the exchange on social media means anything, it means 'they got what they deserved'. The word *karma* means 'action', and though it may seem that karma happens to someone from an external source, as if some outside force is doling out justice or retribution for past deeds or past life actions – this is far from the true Sanskrit meaning of the word, to include how it is used by both Hindus and Buddhists today. Karma is one's inner conditioning and processes that prompt one to experience external consequences; or put simply, one's own life choices. As a Seidwoman, I have observed that those able to 'work through' their karma, are those that, perhaps, would have been recognized as heroes, among the Old European Heathens. Meaning, those who make their own fate / wyrd.

6-Ṛta / Rita, from Proto Indo-European *xártus*, or that which 'fits together; to harmonize, to join rightly; natural order, right order'. Xártus / Ṛta precedes intellectual construction. It is an idea found within *Wyrd Consciousness*, so best understood there. It may be compared / equated to the *Flow* from Audhumla as a Creative Force of All, or *Hvergelmir* – the primal wellspring of All. Additional comparisons may include *wu wei* in Taoism; *samyama* in Hinduism; also, full immersion; hyper-focus; autotelic experience; absorption.

**Conclusion**
*Beseeching, praying, bargaining, each essentially 'begging', are all seen in Judeo-Christian based magics, such as Kabbalah, Ceremonial Magic, Voodoo, and in some instances of Wicca and modern Witchcraft.

*She leads our Craft*

*Matar Geheimnis*

*That Wise Woman*

*Lamp  .  Spirit*

*Woman  .  Creator*